Sally Jones

Bossiney Books

First published in 1984
by Bossiney Books
St Teath, Bodmin, Cornwall
Designed, typeset and printed in Great Britain by
Penwell Ltd, Parkwood, Callington
Cornwall

© *1984 Sally Jones*
ISBN 0 906456 83 5

PLATE ACKNOWLEDGMENTS

Front cover Ray Bishop
Drawings by Paul Honeywill
Julia Davey: pages 5-9, 38, 40, 44, 49, 50-4, 60, 61, 81-4, 87-96,
100-107, 110, back cover.
Peter Friend: pages 12-23, 26, 27, 31, 35-7, 43, 67, 76, 78
Nottingham Castle Museum: page 56
Bath Museums Service: page 63

The Author and Publisher would like to thank the following people
for their help and co-operation: Charles Causley for permission to
use stanzas from 'The Song of Samuel Sweet'; Routledge and Kegan
Paul for permission to quote from *A Sampler of British Folktales* by
Katharine M. Briggs; Mr and Mrs Burge of Doone Valley Riding
Stables, Parsonage Farm, Malmsmead, and Caroline Burge not only
for providing their horse 'Plum' for the author to ride for the cover
photograph but for their help in locations; Major Thomas Trollope-
Bellew of Cromcombe for assistance in placing the Doone legends;
and Lloyd and Philip Walters of Locking Manor for information on
the legend of John Plomley.

About the Author—and the Book

Sally Jones was educated at King Edward VI High School for Girls, Birmingham, and read English at St Hugh's College, Oxford, where she won five Blues—tennis, squash, modern pentathlon, netball and cricket. She was British Schoolgirl tennis champion and has played squash for Devon and tennis and squash for Warwickshire. In 1976 she won the *Sunday Telegraph* writing prize of £500 for an account of a tour of Ireland with the British Universities tennis team. Later she won a prize in the Catherine Pakenham Memorial Awards for Young Women Journalists. In 1978 she joined the BBC as a News Trainee and the following year she moved to Westward TV as a television reporter on Westward Diary.

Since leaving Westward TV in 1981, Sally Jones has worked for HTV (Wales) and Central Television in Birmingham as presenter of their evening news programmes. She has made several documentaries, including one for HTV on the Welsh Horse Trials. But she retains her links with the Westcountry and makes regular trips to Somerset and Devon to ride and research books and articles. She also works as a freelance TV reporter for ITN in London and contributes articles to many newspapers, including the *Sunday Times,* the *Daily Mail* and the *Daily Express.*

Here in *Legends of Somerset,* Sally Jones travels across rich legendary landscapes. 'The legendary place,' she writes, 'is like an object of pilgrimage which commands its devotees "Come and find me".' Words, drawings and photographs all combine to evoke a spirit of adventure.

'However,' she reflects, 'you can get more than just adventure from searching out the legendary places . . . the sites are worth a trek for the sense of walking in ancient footsteps—the footsteps of Neolithic man and King Arthur, St Carantoc and the Duke of Monmouth, Saint Joseph of Arimathea and, who knows, perhaps even the footsteps of Christ himself.'

LEGENDS OF SOMERSET

The legends of Somerset are like a game of 'Chinese Whispers' played long ago. First comes the original story, whether a domestic tragedy, like Walford's murder of his pathetic half-witted wife, a great historical event like the Battle of Sedgemoor or the coming of Joseph of Arimathea as tin-trader and missionary.

Over the years, the stories gradually acquire a deeper resonance as the echoes of the original event, far from dying down, continue to rumble and reverberate. The tale is passed on with subtle additions and distortions. Real life being necessarily full of *non sequiturs* and loose ends, the tale-tellers frequently prefer to tie them up with a dramatic flourish, an element of fantasy or even a rustic joke. The account of the Gurt Vurm of Shervage Wood, for example, is quite hilarious.

Apart from the extra detail acquired through humorous additions, the events themselves continue to generate an energy of their own. It seems from hundreds of testimonies and eye-witness accounts that the battle of Sedgemoor has in some way produced a ripple on the ether, as if the high emotion, the pain and desperation surrounding it, have imprinted themselves on the places where the tragic events were played out.

Just as at scores of sites like Edge Hill and Glencoe a tangible sense of terror remains and the sights and sounds of battle recur as if the whole event were being re-run time and again over the centuries on a hazy and faintly out-of-focus projector. Many of the people living near Sedgemoor accept as a matter of fact that, from time to time, they hear the hooves of a troop of 'King' Monmouth's

The stones at Stanton Drew ... wedding guests turned to stone for dancing on the Sabbath. ▶

4

men cantering along an ancient track en route to the slaughter.

Such experiences seem most accessible to psychics and those sympathetic to another world and it is easy to dismiss them as the working of a well-informed imagination or the effect of drifting shapes produced by marshland mist. All the same, the fact that so many stolid non-believers with no previous knowledge of the battle have yet been granted a 'ringside seat' suggests there is far more to the accounts than this.

I believe that, although we do not yet understand the process, certain events can be replayed, often in the presence of several people. The episodes are usually those of highest tension: the flight from the battlefield, the young girl mourning her sweetheart, the champion runner betrayed by King James's men. It is as if some spiritual tremor has shivered down the ages and made itself felt where the veil is thinnest, often on the same night of the year and at the same time as the original event. Those who have had this experience claim that the most striking effect is frequently an overwhelming sense of dread or pathos that accompanies the vision. It is as if the involuntary witnesses share the emotional burden of those who enact their grief and terror again and again, keeping memories of the event alive and adding to its store of hearsay and legend.

Other folktales carry a far greater element of fantasy. The many stories of dragons, though partly based on sightings of water snakes in the Somerset marshes, can also be seen as a potent metaphor for the Viking raids which may have passed into folk-memory embodied in the fire-breathing predators. Legends such as that of St Carantoc taming the dragon are good stories but also carry a strong religious message and are often read as a parable for the defeat of paganism by Christianity.

In the same way, many of the groups of standing stones, some erected 2,000 years before Christ, are yet held up as examples of divine wrath. The stones at Stanton Drew are said to be the remains of a wedding-party turned to stone for dancing on the Sabbath to the music of a sinister gentleman who steps in when the god-fearing fiddler refuses to play after midnight. Some modern-day cynics say

The Author at the Wimblestone. 'The beauty of the Somerset legends is that so many sites are still visible, whether as standing stones or ancient strongholds.' ▶

he was a member of the musician's union but I prefer to think that his refusal to keep playing was dictated by piety. In Puritan times, the spectacular group of stones would have provided a stern warning to the gadabouts and gladdened the hearts of the Lord's Day Observance Society.

The beauty of the Somerset Legends is that so many of their sites are still visible, whether as standing stones or ancient strongholds. The hill-fort of Cadbury Castle, which many claim is the legendary Camelot where King Arthur held court, is still impressive over fifteen hundred years later.

The legends themselves abound, many in a number of different forms, and selection is the most difficult job. I chose the most spine-tingling I could find, whether they were macabre and bloodthirsty like the tales of the murderous Doones of Badgworthy or holy and awe-inspiring like the account of the Beast's Thorn.

I have used the old pre-1974 boundaries to define the Somerset covered in this book. So many of the places which now fall into the misbegotten hybrid known as Avon seem to me still to have more in

An expanse of water is often the scene of great legend.

Winter sky over Somerset.

common with their old county of Somerset, that I feel justified in this reactionary indulgence.

These days, some of the sites stand in the most modern settings, beside housing estates or petrol stations. The M5 cuts rudely across the old Pilgrim's Way to Glastonbury, a fascinating meeting of the ways and clash of cultures.

A good Ordnance Survey map is vital as it marks most sites, even those that are now almost forgotten. The row of small stones known as Swayne's Leaps in Loxley Woods near Street are a good example. They are a monument to an athletic prisoner who leapt to freedom after being captured at the Battle of Sedgemoor. Now almost entirely overgrown with ivy and brambles, they are hard to find, but the sheer delight of discovery makes the whole search worthwhile.

The legendary place is like an object of pilgrimage which commands its devotees 'Come and find me'. The more testing the goal, the greater the reward for the pilgrim who achieves it. A local farmer said he had once taken a party of American tourists to the

9

spot and heard them exclaim: 'If this were America, the ground round those stones would be mown and the stones properly signposted.' No doubt with a hamburger joint installed into the bargain! To me, the fact that the stones are so well-hidden makes their discovery far more of an adventure than any visit to an Americanised 'Swayne's Leaps Leisure Area' could ever be.

However, you can get far more than just adventure from searching out the legendary places. Like Swayne's Leaps, the sites are worth a trek for the sense of walking in ancient footsteps—the footsteps of Neolithic man and King Arthur, St Carantoc and the Duke of Monmouth, Saint Joseph of Arimathea and, who knows, perhaps even the footsteps of Christ himself.

Here be Dragons

In the days when dank and dangerous marshes covered much of Somerset, it was easy to believe in dragons. The vast tracts of reed and rush gave them cover and the smoke and flame from their breath mingled with the mist that rose from the bogs. Some dragons guarded great heaps of treasure and some preyed on human flesh, showing a marked preference for children. Where they came from, no-one knew, for only once was a dragon ever seen as it formed.

This was the famous Norton Fitzwarren dragon which arose from a heap of bodies at the Iron Age encampment there after a fierce battle. Many still believe that the combination of seething hatred and rotting corpses generated the dragon through a form of spontaneous combustion. Soon all the villagers fled screaming as the scaly beast carried off their children in his jaws and scorched their corn or swooped down to snatch their sheep and goats.

Although life had become intolerable for the country people, anyone with a taste for fairy stories will know that the evildoers are never allowed to get away with it and for every dragon there is always a St George. In this case, a young man called Fulke Fitzwarren fitted the bill and took on the dragon in single combat. After

St Carantoc and the Dragon: ' . . . the bog parted amid yellow sulphurous fumes and a scaly beast appeared, roaring not in rage but in devotion.' ▶

Far left: The rood screen in All Saints Church tells the story of the Norton Fitzwarren dragon. Perhaps the bench end in Crowcombe Church (left) illustrates the same tale.

a long and bloody struggle, he pierced the dragon to the heart and cut off its head.

Although some say that tales of dragons were simply a metaphor for the Danish raids, the legend is now deeply woven into local consciousness. A fine sixteenth-century rood screen in All Saints Church at Norton Fitzwarren tells the story in colourful if sometimes obscure detail. A line of figures carved with tremendous vigour and inventiveness flows and gambols across the six-inch band at the base of the screen. This was once brightly painted but in the nineteenth century a top coat of light oak varnish was applied and the colours are only now beginning to show through once more. Incredibly the screen was later dismantled and in 1886, the rector rescued it in the face of strong local opposition from a Taunton junk-shop.

A letter to the *Gentleman's Magazine* in 1829 describes the scene: 'The first dog is a greyhound; the other two are hounds, one yellow, the other black. Next is a man in a yellow jerkin with red hose and

13

A flying dragon terrorised the marshes near Carhampton.

cap holding in his left hand a circular implement. He seems either on the point of falling a sacrifice to the monster or attempting to entrap him. The animal is carved with great spirit and is painted black with a golden stripe on his back.

'A man next represented with a bow in his hand seems to be making his escape. The figure which is next appears to be meant for a female. Her hands are in an attitude of prayer. She seems a resigned victim of the black monster which is in the act of devouring her.'

Seen directly from below, the figure seemed to me unquestionably meant for a male. His legs have already disappeared into the maw of a bulging reptile like a crocodile, with every scale painstakingly picked out. The other dragon to the left of the screen seems almost alive, his face contorted into a snarl that gives him the appearance of a malevolent bearded lynx. I should certainly back him in any free-for-all with the man in the yellow jerkin.

14

The letter to the magazine also points out three other naked figures and modestly describes their somewhat lewd actions as 'difficult to interpret'. He was obviously just the sort of gentleman the magazine was aimed at.

A carved bench end in Crowcombe Church shows two men assiduously killing a plump, cheery-looking dragon with two heads. It is perhaps the same one that terrorised Norton Fitzwarren, but rendered less than impressive by constraints of space.

St Carantoc and the Dragon

Not all dragons came to a sticky end, however, and the great flying serpent that stalked the marshes around Carhampton was reformed and sent away without a single harsh word. At that time the young King Arthur ruled the country round Dunster in alliance with a chieftain called Catho. The evangelist St Carantoc came to the Westcountry asking God where he should set up his mission. He cast his miraculous marble altar into the Severn Estuary, vowing that he would build a church wherever the great slab of stone came to rest.

Some days later, King Arthur was riding across the marshes on the way to Carhampton. A flying dragon was terrorising the district and had already carried off hundreds of men and devastated the crops. The local people had begged for Arthur's aid because they believed he was the only man who could defeat the reptile.

As he reached the shore, the King saw a mysterious circle of richly-veined marble, shaped like a table, floating in the shallows. He commanded his men to bring it to land and saw engraved on it in a strange script 'The Altar of St Carantoc'. King Arthur covered the great slab and rode on.

A few miles further on, he met St Carantoc, a strange unworldly figure with long white hair streaming over his shoulders. The Saint stopped the King and his retinue with one glance. 'My Lord. Tell me truly, have you seen the altar of St Carantoc?' Arthur was intrigued and thinking that this might be a sorcerer, he asked the old man who he was.

'I am St Carantoc,' the Saint answered gently and Arthur bared his head, realising he was in the presence of holiness.

'I will strike a bargain with you,' he said. 'Call up the dragon from

15

within whatever dank thicket or marsh he is lying and I shall restore your altar.'

St Carantoc nodded silently and turned away in prayer, uttering a strange incantation over the swamp. At once, the slimy tract heaved and the bog parted amid yellow sulphurous fumes and a hideous smell of bad eggs. The King's retinue backed away in horror but Arthur stood his ground as a thickset, scaly beast appeared, roaring not in rage but in devotion. It trotted up to St Carantoc like a calf to its mother, bending its head dutifully as if waiting to be blessed at the altar rail.

The Saint gave a prayer of thanks and fastened his stole about the great, bull-like neck. The crimson material only just encompassed it but St Carantoc led the great serpent with a light hand at the head of a joyful procession up to the court of King Catho at Dunster Castle. His guards drew their swords in fear and one tried to kill the dragon but St Carantoc reassured them that it was quite harmless.

King Catho received them kindly and St Carantoc then led the dragon out and released it back into the marshes, ordering it gently never to harm anyone again. The dragon bowed its head as if it understood and wandered meekly away. It was so transformed by the Saints' prayers that it immediately became a vegetarian and despite its huge size and fearsome appearance, the villagers grew to love it as a pet. Where once it had scorched whole wheatfields with its fiery breath, it now produced the flames only when needed for useful domestic tasks like lighting bonfires in the rain.

As for St Carantoc, Arthur granted him twelve portions of land by the river mouth at Carhampton where the altar had come to rest and here the Saint built a small stone oratory. A chapel stood on the site of the oratory until the sixteenth century in what is now the garden of the old vicarage, a big square house of red sandstone, near the present church.

In some versions, the King takes the great circular slab of marble back to Camelot as his Round Table. The dragon lives on in church carvings at St Decuman and Cleeve.

The Minehead Sailors' 'Oss

Some say that St Carantoc's taming of the dragon describes Christianity defeating paganism. A few brave souls even suggest that the

16

Minehead Sailors' 'Oss which bobs through the streets while its attendants entrap passers-by and demand money each May Day represents not a horse but a dragon. They claim the custom evolved in memory of some enterprising Somerset sailors who disguised their boat as a sea-serpent to frighten off the Norse raiders. This may seem a shade far-fetched but although the effigy with its tail of rope and ribbons does not look much like a sea-serpent, it certainly doesn't look much like a horse either. Records show that up to 1880 the 'Oss possessed a head with snapping jaws to bite those who didn't pay up—perhaps reminiscent of a serpentine past.

The Gurt Vurm of Shervage Wood

A few miles from Minehead on the northern edge of the Quantock Hills comes the jocular folktale of the Gurt Vurm of Shervage

Dunster Castle: ' . . . the young King Arthur ruled the country round Dunster . . .'

Wood. The folklorist Katharine Briggs recounts a hilarious dialect version collected from a local story-teller. Some passages show delightful flashes of dry Somerset wit.

The 'Vurm', a massive serpent-like creature, lived in Shervage Wood. It slept most of the day with its huge bulk coiled round the trees of the old camp. It was as thick as three oak trees and like most monsters, it lived on human flesh. A daring shepherd and two Stowey broom-squires ventured near its lair and were never seen again. It crushed any sheep and cattle that came within range then swallowed them whole before going back to sleep again. Even the wild ponies that usually cropped quietly in the woods, disappeared mysteriously and the farmers were furious because there were none to sell at Bridgwater Fair.

Gradually the vurm's food supplies began to run out. It had eaten all the ponies and the wary farmers now guarded their herds closely on the lower slopes. Even the deer and rabbits had moved across to Hurley Beacon. No-one dared to set foot within a mile of the wood, not even those who usually made their living there. Worst hit was an old woman who lived in Crowcombe at the foot of the Quantocks. She earned a few pence a day picking worts or bilberries and making them into tarts to sell at the Triscombe Revel and she was tortured by the thought of all the ripe fruit going to waste.

Then a stranger arrived in Crowcombe, a woodman with an open jaunty manner. He befriended the old lady and she persuaded him to go up to Shervage Wood, supposedly to see if the worts were ripe. He agreed and she packed him a bundle of bread and cheese and a drop of cider to see him through the day. The dialect account continues:

> Being a Stogumber stranger (Stogumber is about three miles from Crowcombe!) he wan't used to Quantock Hills and by the time he'd a-walked into Shervage Wood and seed a wonderful fine lot of worts on the way, he were feeling 'twere quite time for his cider.
>
> He'd just got nicely started on his mummet when the log begins to squirmy about under'n.
>
> 'Hold a bit!' says he picking up his axe. 'Thee do movey do thee? Take that then.' And he raised axe and cut it in two and both ends of the log began to bleed. Then the one end it up and run as hard as it could go to Bilbrook and t'other end it runned to

Kingston St Mary and since they two halves went t'wrong way to meet, the gurt vurm couldn't nowise grow together again so her died.

Folks down to Bilbrook, they call their place Dragon Cross and folk to Kingston St Mary, they boasts about the same old tale of a fiery dragon—might be as they got the head end of our gurt vurm—but he were all Quantock to start with.

After the two ends had disappeared, the woodman finished his meal and walked back to Crowcombe, carrying a hatful of ripe worts for the old woman, deeply suspicious that he had been kept in the dark.

'There were a dragon there, fust go off,' he tells her, very thoughtful. But all 'er says is

'Didn't 'ee know. Didn' someone tell 'ee?' (all innocence.)

The tale ends with a touch of tight-lipped comedy.

'Her were a Crowcombe woman,' as if this explained a lot.

The Dragon of Aller

Another famous Somerset dragon devastated the village of Aller. It was a monstrous flying serpent which breathed flames and dark poisonous fumes and seemed utterly invulnerable because of its thick scaly armour. Apart from human flesh, it loved fresh milk and would bear down on laden milkmaids and drain the full pails or suck dry the cows in the fields, leaving them such scraggy, shaking creatures that most never gave another drop.

But John Aller, a gallant knight who lived nearby, came to the rescue. He plastered his body with pitch and put on a thick mask so that the dragon's fiery breath couldn't harm him. He took a long, graceful spear specially carved for the conflict and climbed up to the dragon's den, attacking it while it slept.

The fight that followed was long and deadly. The dragon singed whole patches of the hillside as it tried to scorch its enemy but John Aller was too quick for it and suffered only minor burns. At last, as the dragon shook its head from side to side, gathering itself for a final onslaught, John Aller grasped his spear and drove it straight into its heart. Flaming blood ran out and blackened the whole

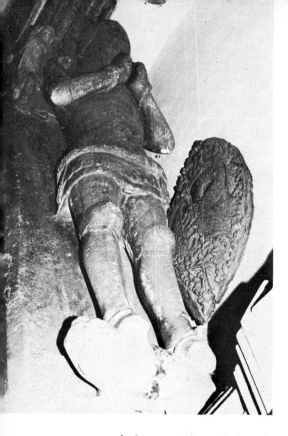

Left: ' . . . the defaced effigy
of a knight with nose and feet
missing in Aller Church . . .'
Right: The Author tries out
John Aller's spear at Low
Ham Church.

area and the great beast's last breath rose upwards like a pall of
dense smoke.

John Aller tiptoed into the dark lair and found two or three baby
dragons there, each as fierce as its father. He rushed home and
fetched labourers to stop up the hole with the spikes of a solid iron
harrow so that the evil brood starved to death; hence the slightly
inaccurate rhyme, 'The Dragon of Aller was killed by a harrow.'

Another version of the story says that John Aller was a peasant
who was so badly burned by the dragon's breath that he and the
monster fell dead at the same instant and that the village then took
his name to commemorate his courage.

All the same, I prefer the more aristocratic story and like to think
that the defaced effigy of a knight with nose and feet missing in
Aller Church was indeed John Aller, the dragon-killer. Certainly the
knight is still well-armed with a dagger hanging by cords from his
baldric, though his famous spear is now kept in Low Ham Church, a
long slender dart, nine feet long with a businesslike metal tip. The

shaft is painted in faded bands of brown, green and yellow, divided by black rings, and it feels light and well-balanced, like a good javelin, long and sharp enough to pierce a dragon's hide.

The Beast of Exmoor

'A hound it was; an enormous coal-black hound, but not such a hound as mortal eyes have ever seen. Fire burned from its open mouth, its eyes glowed with a smouldering glare, its muzzle and hackles and dewlap were outlined in flickering flame.'

Eighty years after Sherlock Holmes and Dr Watson set eyes on the hellish hound of the Baskervilles, another savage killer roams the moors of the Westcountry. As if to prove that fresh legends are evolving all the time, the beast of Exmoor stalks like a latter-day dragon, devouring lambs and slaughtering sheep with impunity. It roams the moorlands and through the Sunday newspapers beneath

21

banner headlines—'Beast strikes again', 'Army foxed'—the perfect silly season story and enough to get half the journalists in Fleet Street out and stumbling over the moors in unsuitable shoes. In this mundane fashion, modern legends are made.

The local farmers and Royal Marine marksmen stalking the beast of course demand a rational explanation. Their theories so far include a rogue Alsatian, a wolf, a puma and even a black panther.

In the Exmoor villages, however, the beast has already taken on a supernatural dimension, a Satanic creature in the time-honoured tradition of spectral black dogs. Only a handful of people claim even a glimpse of it but most say they saw a thickset black animal bounding swiftly over the heather. Most disturbing of all is its ability to vanish like a ghost within seconds of making its kill and under the very noses of those lying in wait to catch it.

The farmers have formed armed posses to beat through woodlands. Military marksmen with sophisticated night sights have hunted it in vain. Even a dozen trackers and two clairvoyants have had no luck.

One farmer who has lost fifty sheep fears the worst: 'We're dealing with something extraordinary here. It's as if he's got a human brain.' Others claim to have seen the beast jump two high hedges thirty feet apart in one bound. Like the Hound of the Baskervilles the beast possesses an unearthly scream and one old shepherd described it as 'more like a soul in torment than any mortal creature I ever heard'.

Since March 1983, the beast has notched up an impressive tally of over a hundred sheep and lambs, many with their throats ripped out cleanly as if killed for pleasure. All this but most of all the chilling cry is enough to confer legendary status, at least until some enterprising wolf or puma escaped from a circus meets the Marines face-to-face for a last showdown.

The Doones

The human forerunners of the beast of Exmoor were certainly the Doones, the evil family who once terrorised the isolated farms and villages around Badgworthy. They did not confine their attentions to sheep, however, and many of the tales about them tell of the sadistic pleasure they took in pillage and murder.

Although the family really existed, it was R.D. Blackmore's powerful novel, *Lorna Doone*, which first brought them widespread notoriety and it is now difficult to separate the strands of truth and exaggeration from entire fiction. Certainly Blackmore's version captured the public's imagination, particularly the great feud between the deep-dyed villain, Carver Doone, and the hero, John Ridd, himself a real person who, like his fictional namesake, went to Blundell's School, Tiverton.

According to the book, the Doones were aristocrats, protected from the law by their ancient ancestry. They fell on hard times and lost their land and possessions before turning to lives of crime, lives so evil that to modern ears, their black deeds can sound unintentionally comic. It is difficult nowadays to take cannibalism seriously, though it was obviously a real threat to the young Jan Ridd as he crouched above the track, watching the evil brood riding home, silhouetted against the flames of Dunkery Beacon:

Doone Country: '... its sheer grandeur remains the best guardian of these deep-rooted legends ...'

'The horsemen passed in silence, scarcely deigning to look round; heavy men and large of stature, reckless how they bore their guns or how they sate their horses with leathern jerkins and long boots and iron plates on breast and head, plunder heaped behind their saddles and flagons slung in front of them.

'More than thirty went along like clouds upon red sunset. Some had carcases of sheep swinging with their skins on, others had deer and one had a child flung across his saddle-bow. Whether the child were dead or alive was beyond my vision, only it hung head downwards and must take the chance of it. They had got the child, a very young one, for the sake of the dress no doubt which they would not stop to pull off from it, for the dress shone bright where the fire struck it as if with gold and jewels. I longed in my heart to know most sadly what they would do with the little thing and whether they would eat it.'

Images like that die hard and no wonder tourists still visit the village of Oare to see the window from where Carver Doone shot Lorna at the altar.

The real Doones were probably Scottish freebooters who came to live in the lonely valley along Haccombe Water. They would certainly have poached more than their share of sheep and deer and were probably not averse to shooting down anyone who tried to prevent them, so no farm or homestead within a night's ride of Badgworthy would have been safe. They kept one step ahead of the Devon and Somerset militias by simply dodging over the appropriate county boundary when one or other band came in search of them.

Despite their actual misdemeanours, the myth far outstripped the reality in sheer, spine-chilling evil. The legendary Doones evidently gloried in slaughter and in their hideous reputation. On one occasion they were looting a house belonging to their arch-enemies and decided to wipe out anyone they could find. They captured the young daughter but could see no sign of her mother who was hiding inside the great oven. Slowly and sadistically the Doones drew back the child's head and slit her throat, remarking sardonically:

'Kill the calf and the cow will howl.' Their prediction was correct

'The horsemen passed in silence . . . one had a child flung across his saddle bow.'▶

Above: A bridge near the Doone Valley. Right: Oare Church where Lorna Doone was shot on her wedding day.

and the anguished mother burst from the oven only to meet the same fate herself.

The final outrage came when, after killing a baby, they rode away leaving a mocking message sprawled on a placard round its neck:

'If anyone ax thee who killed thee,
   Say 'twere the Doones o' Badgery!'

The two county militias for once combined, mobilised a huge force and marched on the Doone's stronghold, bristling with billhooks, clubs and muskets. Most of the clan were killed in the pitched battle that followed and the rest were hanged, drawn and quartered.

The last time I visited Doone Valley, I took the marked footpath from near Brendon Two Gates on the A3223 between Simonsbath and the north coast. It was autumn with driving rain and a light veil of mist along the tops of the smooth ridges of moorland. The nearest were clearly outlined as sharp horizontal lines but each fold became increasingly blurred in the hazy middle distance as if a painter had

smeared his finger across the horizon until it was impossible to see where moor finished and sky began. The wind hurtled me along the deserted track through the dying heather and bracken. This was the weather to bring out the full menace of Doone country, not the unthreatening high summer in a landscape full of tourists. At any moment I expected to hear galloping hooves or catch a glimpse of Jan Ridd and Carver in their deadly struggle beside Wizard Slough.

Oare Church was far more welcoming, full of the grapes, hops and wheatsheaves of Harvest Festival. I lingered at the spot where Lorna was shot on her wedding day. She would have been standing about half-way up the church, not at the present altar since that section was a more recent addition. She would certainly have been an easy target for Carver, taking aim through the middle window, just a few feet away.

The area has changed little in hundreds of years and its sheer grandeur remains the best guardian of these deep-rooted legends of brutality and the power of love over evil.

The Devil in Somerset

If the Doones terrified the local people, the Devil was a more potent threat still. Many would have consoled themselves with the thought that the wicked gang would eventually meet their match bound for damnation. The Somerset tales of the Devil are certainly strongest on Exmoor and the Quantocks. The combination of wild, isolated conditions and fire and brimstone from the pulpit every Sunday must have made perdition seem a very real possibility.

Certain places were known to be possessed, including Tarr Steps, the ancient bridge over the River Barle near Simonsbath. The Devil reputedly built it for his own use and one rash cat which ventured across was torn to pieces on the spot. Then a local priest tried to rid the bridge of its Satanic creator, who argued the toss in playground insults:

'You're a black crow!'

'I'm no blacker than the Devil,' rejoined the priest and his

◄The Wish-Hounds are 'the spirits of the damned, baying in eternal torment'.

adversary vanished in a puff of black smoke. It is comforting to know that the Devil can be so easily outwitted.

As on Dartmoor, Satan is often pictured as the demon huntsman on a strange black steed, at his heels a pack of Wish-Hounds with tongues of red flame. They are the spirits of the damned, baying in eternal torment.

The Devil hunts his quarry of human souls, thundering along the ancient tracks and to see or hear the Wild Hunt brings terrible misfortune unless you are riding a horse shod with iron shoes. The pack has been known to venture down off the hills and a dark hunts-man was once seen waiting under trees in a lane near Combwich. The next day, the local witch woman was found dead. The Devil had come to collect his own.

All the same, the hills remained the biggest danger. The Quantock people always avoided the Triscombe stone on stormy nights 'when the hounds might be running' and anyone who heard them coming would rush for cover in the bushes. Even now if you cross the crown of the Quantocks on a blustery night, it is easy to imagine the infernal hound music above the scream of the wind through the beech avenues or fancy that beyond the shaggy moorland ponies huddled among the silver birches gallops a shadowy figure on a headless horse.

The Danish Minstrel of Dowsborough

The Devil occasionally descended to more mundane means of trans-port and he sometimes materialised near Dowsborough Camp, riding a black pig. Dowsborough, the second highest of the Quan-tock Hills, is the site of an Iron Age fort and was once called Danesborough after a battle in which a party of marauding Danes was wiped out. Some say that their ghosts live on beneath the hill. Farmworkers plodding home late to Dodington and Nether Stowey claim they have heard sounds of revelry, drunken laughter and singing or the shouts of battle and weird horn-music together with an inexplicable sense of foreboding as if the fatal last battle were imprinted for eternity.

One young man's tragic story lives on. He was a Danish minstrel with no stomach for battle, who ran away before the fighting started. He met a local girl, the village beauty, who sheltered him

'The Quantock people always avoided
the Triscombe Stone on stormy nights
when the hounds might be running . . .'

and the two fell in love. After the slaughter, the Somerset men combed the area for survivors and discovered the young minstrel. His lover's tears and pleading were in vain and he was put to death. His ghost still wanders among the brown scrub oak on the Dowsborough slopes, mournfully plucking at his harp and singing in a voice infinitely faint and far away.

Wordsworth must have heard the tale during his time at Nether Stowey for he writes of the melancholy spirit with his fur vest and harp who

> warbles songs of war
> That seem like songs of love.

Even today the slopes of Dowsborough between Lady's Combe and Butterfly Combe are known simply as Dead Boy.

The Low Ham Fiddler

Another minstrel who did rather better from his skill was the fiddler of Low Ham, famous throughout the district for his lively playing at all the local hops. At the time, the village was owned by Lord Stawell, a by-word for extravagance. He even sold off several manors to pay for his riotous living and grandiose alterations to his great house. Despite his self-indulgence he was a harsh landlord and his tenants shrank from him.

One Christmas Eve the fiddler was trudging home from a dance around midnight when a rich gentleman's carriage stopped beside him and a tall figure in a black cloak stepped across his path.

'Are you the famous fiddler of Low Ham?' he asked with a strange leer. For a second the fiddler fancied he heard a faint roar like far-off flames, but he saw not a trace of fire and answered steadily enough:

'Folks round here do call me that sir.'

'Will you then play for the ball at my house tomorrow night. I shall fetch you myself and you will be well rewarded—with good red gold, no less,' and the gentleman's smile revealed pointed teeth like

**The Danish Minstrel 'still wanders on the Dowsborough slopes . . .
mournfully plucking at his harp . . . his voice
infinitely faint . . .' ▶**

the fangs of a wolf. The fiddler hesitated but he thought of the gold which would transform his family's poor celebrations and at last agreed.

As the gentleman had promised, the coach met him at the same spot the next night. After a long twisting drive with the blinds down, they reached a fine house blazing with lights and full of laughing revellers; beautiful women in brocade and cloth of gold, bright jewels at throat and wrist. When he played, the stately company danced, flowing, intricate measures such as he had never seen. He played faster and the room seemed to spin round in a kaleidoscope of colour.

The dance went on into the early hours of the morning and at last the joyful revellers crowded round, applauding him and pressing gold pieces into his hand. His host took him by the arm and led him around the magnificent house, through rooms hung with tapestry and paved with marble and at last into the most splendid bedroom of all. The fiddler gazed at the great gold bed in awe but noticed a strange smell of burning. He touched the bedstead and leapt back. It was boiling hot as if a fire were burning underneath. His companion smiled grimly.

'This is the bed I have prepared for the evil Lord Stawell. He will get but fitful sleep for all eternity. Come, my coachman will drive you home—but take care to breathe no word of what you have seen or great harm will befall you.'

As the fiddler said his farewells laden with gold, he noticed that one of his host's feet was misshapen, almost as if he had tried to cram a cloven hoof into the elegant scarlet shoe. The fiddler's suspicions were confirmed but despite his terror, he went straight to Lord Stawell to warn him that he stood in mortal danger of hell-fire.

At first his lordship scoffed but after one glance at the gold, he became pale and thoughtful. The fiddler went home and threw the gold coins into a ditch. Next morning they had turned to dry leaves but in their place came a bag of gold from Lord Stawell who was already mending his ways. He built almshouses and cottages for the poor and made sure all his tenants were well fed. As for the fiddler, he and his family lived in prosperity for the rest of their lives and the fiery bed remained empty.

Devil's Stone at Staple Fitzpaine. ▶

Castle Neroche (left) . . . a wonderful vantage point for the Devil.
The lower ramparts (above) have a strangely eerie atmosphere.

Castle Neroche

Perhaps the fine gentleman's house was built on the commanding
stronghold of Castle Neroche near Staple Fitzpaine. Certainly the
Devil is credited with making his headquarters there to give himself
maximum scope for attacking the surrounding villages. At one
stage, his onslaughts took the form of stone-throwing on a massive
scale, directed against the church in Staple Fitzpaine. He hurled
three huge boulders from the summit of the ancient hill fort Castle
Neroche. Luckily for the parishioners, all three fell short, landing
harmlessly along the lane leading down into the village. These were
known as the Devil's Stones or Sarcen Stones.

Some also called them the Devil's Jumps and said they marked three mighty leaps the Devil made from the castle down towards the village, running out of steam just before the church.

Whatever the origin of the stones, the biggest now stands in the grounds of Taunton Museum but another is still just visible beside the road above the church. A local woman showed me the great stone on the left hand side of the road running up from the village towards Castle Neroche, 400 yards above the church. It is now half-covered with ivy and brambles but still unmistakable, lying beside the hedge in a landscape otherwise free of boulders, a smooth, rounded expanse like a half millstone with a curious niche in the centre.

Castle Neroche itself is well worth a visit, rearing up in a great tree-covered mound above the Vale of Taunton and the patchwork of fields stretching to the sea. The earthwork of ditches and banks that formed the castle's lower ramparts is still impressive with a strangely eerie atmosphere despite its alternative function as a scrambling-ground for the local motorbike boys. The summit of the castle must have provided a wonderful vantage point for the Devil. Perhaps it was only shortage of stones that stopped him scoring a

Cows encountered whilst looking for the Wimblestone.

direct hit on the church—or perhaps it was the sheer misery of the freezing winter in which he's said to have died of cold. According to legend, he now lies buried under Windwhistle Hill, so the Staple Fitzpaine churchgoers are safe.

The Treasure Stones of Somerset

Although the Devil is no longer in residence, Castle Neroche still contains hidden treasure they say, possibly Old Nick's life-savings hidden beneath the hill. As with most ill-gotten gains, anyone who tries to make his fortune digging for the gold usually meets an unpleasant end. Like the curse of Tutankhamen, tales of death and disaster befalling treasure-seekers were designed to deter would-be robbers who might desecrate sacred sites.

In 1854, the Reverend F. Warre drew a gleeful moral from a ghoulish tale of retribution:

'About 100 years ago, a number of labouring men, urged on by the love of filthy lucre and not having the fear of archaeological societies before their eyes, with sacrilegious spade and pick axe, violated the sanctity of this mysterious hill. But before they found a single coin, they were seized with a panic fear, renounced their presumptuous enterprise and wonderful and awful to relate, within one month of the commencement of their enterprise, some by accident, some by sudden death and some by violent fevers, all paid with their lives the penalty of their covetous and most presumptuous attempt.

'Oh! That this most veracious legend were universally published as a warning to all wanton mutilators of ancient earthworks.'

So let that be a lesson to you!

The Wimblestone

The Wimblestone which stands near Shipham in the Mendips is also said to conceal a great horde of gold. As at Castle Neroche anyone who tries to dig for the treasure runs the risk of terrible misfortune. The stone occasionally deserts its post as guardian of the gold for the unlikely and frivolous pursuit of dancing—but the dancing nights are few and far between.

An old man, Zebedee Fry, was on his way back from haymaking on Midsummer's Eve when he sensed a huge dark bulk, rustling along the hedge. He was terrified and threw himself down in fear. Peeping through shaking fingers he saw the whole field in bright moonlight and the Wimblestone, hopping and tripping with ponderous grace. In the place where the stone usually stood, a pile of bright stones glittered in the moonlight. Zebedee's eyes widened with greed but then his fear overcame him again. He uttered a strangled shriek, took to his heels and didn't stop running until he reached the safety of the Shipham Inn.

Of course his friends scoffed and called him a fool for not filling his pockets while he had the chance. He thoughtfully sipped his pint however and reflected that if his friends had been in his shoes and seen the great mass skipping and dancing so nimbly, they too might have run for their lives and not stayed to make their fortune.

The Wimblestone can at times take a perverse delight in staying

The Wimblestone: ' . . . hopping and tripping with ponderous grace.'

put. A farmer once harnessd his two strongest shire horses to the stone and spent an entire day vainly trying to topple it. The horses heaved until the sweat ran down their flanks—but to no avail. Next he himself stepped into the yoke with them and strained until he too could hardly stand. All the time the stone never moved and as dusk fell the farmer and his team tottered away in deep disgust.

The moment they were out of sight, the Wimblestone creaked out of position and started stumping across the moors. It roamed the hills all night and even visited the Waterstone at Wrington to tell it all about the farmer's stupidity.

The Wimblestone is marked on Ordnance Survey maps near the hamlet of Star. It is very difficult to find, standing in one of the tiny fields which slice the flat plain into a green chequerboard. The land is private and none of the locals, including two youths chopping wood nearby, knew the stone's whereabouts. Few had even heard of it.

From across the field, the flat slab looks like an ancient gravestone and communicates an atmosphere of peace and sanctity as if its presence somehow made the landscape complete. Although it appears immovable, it is delightful to imagine it sneaking off for a few hours romp over the moors before dawn.

Like the Wimblestone, Ham Stone which stands on Ham Hill near the Dorset border was of a convivial nature and enjoyed an evening ramble down to its local. An old rhyme in the district ran:

When Ham Stone hears the Norton chimes at midnight clack,
It rolls down to drink at the Jack O'Beards and back.

For the Cockcrow Stone at Wellington, the signal to move came at dawn with the first cock crow. Then the stone would roll aside to reveal the heap of gold beneath it. All the same any early risers who decide to sit it out in the hope of riches will be in for a long wait for 'it must be the right dawn and the right cock', and who's to say when those two conditions will next coincide?

Robin Hood's Leaps

It is just as fruitless to try excavating Robin Hood's Butts, the three round tumuli on the Blackdowns near Staple Hill. Despite scores of tales, the butts are in fact Bronze Age long barrows. They are also said to contain treasure and a rich man who heard this story decided to finance a dig to uncover the gold and add to his wealth.

From the start, nothing went right. Picks were blunted inexplicably. The workmen quarrelled amongst themselves and met with a spate of minor accidents but, worst of all, however much they laboured, there was no trace of their work the next day; a pit dug the night before would be filled in by the time they returned in the morning. The men grew discouraged at making so little progress and one by one they drifted away. The rich man who had started the excavations was forced to call them off, so frustrated that he was almost reduced to tears. After that, everyone learned the hard way that the treasure was there to stay and no-one has tried to dig for it since.

In spite of their picturesque name, the butts are not in fact linked with Robin Hood. According to legend, two warring giants threw great heaps of mud at one another from either side of the hills. They were obviously bad shots because several of the heaps missed their target and fell to earth with a thud, forming the rounded hillocks of the butts.

These days, little of the atmosphere of the fight remains and the site where the two main butts lie a few yards apart is a quiet rather melancholy place with a grove of fine beech trees growing over the grassy mounds. On the grey day I visited them, the cloud was low, white shreds of mist clinging to the tops of the beeches. The whole aura of strangeness was enhanced by scores of bright red toadstools thickly sprinkled around the roots of the trees. The brilliant scarlet fungus was speckled with white dots and the effect was highly dramatic if artificial. The scene only needed a clutch of gnomes to become a Walt Disney fantasy, though no more fantastic than the image of the snarling giants tossing vast handfuls of mud over the Blackdown Hills.

Sir John Popham

Not far from the butts, a real-life giant who became a legend in the district has been inching his way towards salvation for the past four centuries. Sir John Popham was a local landowner and a great politician. He was also exceedingly corrupt and became a byword for vice and deceit.

Popham was born in 1531 at Huntworth near Bridgwater of rich parents. It is said he was stolen by gypsies as a child, though this is perhaps an attempt to explain why he later became such a bad lot, and, if untrue, is a great slur on the travelling people. As a young man, he went to London, supposedly to study Law but this was merely a cover for learning very different skills as the diarist John Aubrey observed:

'He was severall yeares addicted himselfe but little to the studie of the lawes but profligate company and was wont to take a purse with them. His wife considered her and his condition and at last prevailed with him to lead another life.'

He may have been leading 'another life' but it is extremely questionable whether this constituted any improvement. Certainly he cultivated an outward appearance of respectability and his wealth and connections assured him of a rapid rise to the top. In his forties he became Speaker of the House of Commons and later Chief Justice but his character remained less than spotless and accusations of corruption dogged him for the rest of his life. He

Robin Hood's Butts: ' . . . two warring giants threw great heaps of mud at one another . . .'

looked every inch a villain too for a contemporary described him as 'huge as a barrel and grossly ugly'.

All the same, he was forceful and unscrupulous, somehow surviving a damaging scandal when the vast Littlecote estates passed to him unexpectedly on the death of Darrel, their owner, a man with an equally unsavoury reputation. Although nothing was ever proved, Popham had presided over the trial in which Darrel was acquitted of a damning murder charge. Before the trial, every other lawyer declared it was an open-and-shut affair which could only end on the gallows. Popham ignored public opinion and proved them wrong. He was well-rewarded at the time though he rashly ignored the long-term effects on his spiritual well-being and he is still paying the penalty.

One day he was out hunting in Wilscombe Bottom, a narrow combe half a mile west of the Wellington monument. He spurred on his horse recklessly but the animal shied, then bolted forward in terror throwing his rider into a bottomless pool. Popham struck his head and quickly drowned. Then, as a just reward for his evil life, his soul was despatched hot-foot to hell.

His wife who had stood by him throughout his chequered career remained loyal even after his death and prayed steadfastly for his salvation. Despite the blackness of his crimes, her prayers took effect and on New Year's Eve his ghost rose from the pool, condemned to creep towards Wellington Church at the rate of a cockstride a year.

Belief in this snail-like progress still flourished in the last century and in 1859, a group of men chopping down a tree heard piteous shrieks and cries coming from inside it. They dropped their axes and rushed away, convinced that the soul of Sir John Popham had taken temporary refuge in the tree on its way to the church.

The theme of an endless journey or task is a common one, from the tale of Sisyphus endlessly rolling his boulder uphill to Jan Tregeagle, the evil steward of Lanhydrock in Cornwall, vainly weaving a rope of sand. Such legends invariably 'point a moral to adorn a tale' and the story of Popham's journey to redemption is typical. Unfortunately for the moralists, not all the details of the story tally with the historical facts for the real Sir John died in his

◀The tomb of Sir John Popham at Wellington.

bed at the age of 72 and lies buried in state at St John the Baptist's Church in Wellington.

Nonetheless, the combination of contemporary account and colourful myth points to a powerful folk-memory of the evil squire. If he really died a peaceful death, there is probably a strong element of wishful thinking in the tale of penance. Villains cannot be seen to profit from their crimes and even if they flourish like the green bay tree during their lives, justice dictates that they must pay later, in legend if not in fact, hence Popham's achingly slow progress to salvation.

The murderers of St Thomas à Becket

It will take the soul of Sir John Popham a few millenia yet to reach his goal but at least he is on the way. Other less fortunate souls are condemned to suffer throughout eternity for their crimes. The four knights who conspired to murder the 'turbulent priest', Thomas à Becket, at the very altar of Canterbury Cathedral can never expiate their sacrilegious act. After the murder they must have realised that they stood in mortal danger of damnation for two of them endowed churches near Watchet on the north coast of Somerset in an attempt to atone for the outrage.

De Brito gave money to build the church at Sampford Brett; the word itself is a corruption of de Brito. The sinister ringleader Sir Reginald Fitzurse in his turn endowed Williton Church.

Sadly for the murderers, these pious actions were probably in vain, for two of the knights are buried on the island of Flat Holm in the Bristol Channel, their graves lying in unhallowed ground, facing north. Traditionally only those who lie with their feet towards the morning will rise at the Resurrection. At least one of the two knights, Sir William de Tracey, still feels his spiritual exile keenly. He is condemned to leave Flat Holm each day en route to Woolacombe where he must everlastingly make bundles of sand and bind them with rope of the same unsatisfactory material. He cries in anguish as he drifts away and his moaning is the foghorn of Flat

◀Giant Gorm: ' . . . fell to his death in the Bristol Channel with a massive splash.'

47

Holm. He has much to mourn, for Beckett's murder brought down a curse on his whole family and nothing ever prospered for them afterwards. An old rhyme runs: 'All the de Traceys have the wind in their faces.'

Giant Gorm

Long before the time of Becket, the islands of Flat Holm and Steep Holm were formed by murder on a grand scale. A fearsome giant named Gorm lived near Bristol and, according to legend, dragged two great wedges of earth apart to make the Avon gorge. He was a warlike creature and so clumsy that he often crushed people beneath his feet.

When a young giant challenged him to defend his territory he cursed and stamped until the sea raged and the earth shook beneath his feet. He roared and the local people dashed indoors thinking that there was a great storm overhead. The young giant remained calm and breathed evenly as he flexed his muscles. Then the two crashed together, each grappling to get the stronger grip on the other.

All day they wrestled and although Giant Gorm was stronger and heavier, his opponent was more agile and leapt up from many seemingly back-breaking throws. At last he wore down Giant Gorm and reduced him to a shambling hulk, gasping and wheezing for breath. He staggered and the young giant seized his chance, lunging into him and tugging his arm down sharply so that he lost his balance and fell to his death in the Bristol Channel with a massive splash. Over the years his bones have weathered and become the islands of Steep Holm and Flat Holm, fit resting place for the treacherous knights.

The Wedding of Stanton Drew

Such metamorphoses are common although the most typical involve people who are transformed as a punishment. Just south of Bristol, a spectacular monument is still visible, the stone circles at Stanton Drew. Centuries ago one Midsummer's Eve a wedding party was in full swing on this spot. The bride threw back her veil and everyone began dancing to the local fiddler. The wine flowed freely and the fiddler's bow dashed faster and faster across the strings. Bride and groom whirled up and down the sets, eyes sparkling, faces red as fire, while the guests jigged and pranced, drunk with the feverish rhythms of the music.

It was like a drug and no-one noticed that midnight was approaching except for the fiddler, a quiet devout man. At length with the revelry in full swing he put aside the fiddle and approached the bride.

'I'm afraid I must stop playing now for it is almost midnight and tomorrow is the Sabbath Day.'

'Who cares about the Sabbath?' she shrieked. 'This is my wedding and no-one is going to spoil it. Play on fiddler, we'll reward you well enough.'

The guests clustered round: 'Yes, you must keep playing. It seems as if we've hardly started.' They pressed gold coins into his hands but the fiddler was adamant.

Stone Circle at Stanton Drew: ' . . . one Midsummer's Eve a wedding party was in full swing . . .'

Stanton Drew: ' . . . leaving the revellers turned to stone.'

'I cannot take your money for we profane the Lord's Day with dancing. I am sorry to disappoint you but I can play no more.' He packed up his fiddle and started walking home. The bride flew into a fury.

'Why should my party be ruined by that insolent fiddler? We must simply send for someone else to take over, after all no-one will ever know we danced on the Sabbath—and who cares anyway?'

At that moment a tall black-robed stranger appeared as if by magic, carrying a fiddle-case. One foot seemed deformed and he limped slightly as he made his way into the circle of dancers.

'My lady, if you wish to dance, I should be honoured to play for you. My skill is not great but it would be better than nothing and I shall happily play until dawn.' The bride clapped her hands with delight.

'And play you shall,' she ordered. 'Form up the sets again and we shall dance the night away. At least one man round here does not go cap in hand and cowardly at the very mention of the Sabbath.'

Soon they were once more jigging and curtseying but this time no-one could keep still for an instant. The music was high and wild forcing the revellers to dance furiously until they thought their lungs would burst. Then it changed; slower now and more mournful as if a thousand souls were wailing in torment. The dancers longed to stop but the fiddler ignored their cries, tapping to the music with his misshapen foot in its odd black boot.

'You shall dance till dawn as I promised,' he declared with a horrible leer. 'No-one shall say that I go back on my word.'

At the edge of the field, the first fiddler lay, an unwilling onlooker. On his way home he had ducked down by the hedge to get a better look at the man who had taken his place and found he could move neither hand nor foot. Still the dance went on relentlessly until as the first streaks of dawn stained the eastern sky dove-grey, the cloaked musician walked away, leaving the revellers turned to stone. As he reached the edge of the field he paused:

'Wait patiently wedding guests,' he shouted, 'I shall be back to play for you again before long.' He swept off his hat with a low bow revealing two horns amongst his dark curls then vanished with a mocking cackle.

The first fiddler crouching in terror beneath the hedge suddenly regained the use of his limbs and ran to the village where he sobbed out his story. People came from miles around to see the petrified wedding party but all their prayers and entreaties were in vain. The stones have remained in their original formation to this day. So far the Devil has not kept his promise to return—but that is only what you would expect.

Historians claim that the stones were erected by Neolithic man for religious reasons or ceremonial purposes and Dr William Stukeley was positively sniffy about the ancient folk-belief.

'The noble monument is vulgarly called the Weddings and they say 'tis a company that assisted at a nuptial solemnity thus petrified. In an orchard near the church is a cove consisting of three stones like that of the northern circle in Avebury. This they call the parson, his bride and bridegroom.'

The three stones are set close together as if whispering to one another. A short distance away there are three circles and two avenues. The revellers were evidently petrified during one of the old English country dances as they stood clapping in circles and long sets. Nearby is a fallen megalith, perhaps one of the party taking a nap while he waits for the fiddler to strike up again.

I had intended to count the stones but read this account by John Wood and decided not to.

'No-one, say the country people about Stantondrue, was ever able to reckon the Number of these Metamorphosed Stones or take a Draught of them, tho' several have attempted to do both and proceeded until they were either struck dead upon the Spot or with such illness as soon carried them off.'

It seems to me that running the risks involved in counting the stones goes well beyond the author's duty to inform. If readers are desperate for this knowledge, I suggest they try counting themselves and then let me know their findings—if they live to tell the tale, that is.

The Witch of Wookey

A few miles south of Stanton Drew at Wookey Hole stands the figure of a woman who was turned to stone—but by a holy man, not the Devil. She was once an evil witch who lived in the Great Cave of Wookey Hole where she practised the black arts, especially necromancy. She was very beautiful but as she became more and more steeped in wickedness, her eyes became beady and sunken, her teeth fell out and her body grew hunched and twisted. All her spells and black arts could not restore her beauty.

She was furious, bearing a particular grudge against pretty young girls and could hardly bear to see lovers walking hand in hand. One day a pair of newly-weds passed her cave. They looked so happy that she flew into a rage and vowed to break up their marriage.

After long nights of conjuring spirits and directing all the powers of darkness against the couple, the witch triumphed and the once-happy marriage foundered. The young man was heartbroken and became a monk at Glastonbury Abbey, determined to overcome the evil woman who had destroyed his marriage.

A few years later, local villagers rebelled against the witch's reign of terror and sent messengers to the Abbot of Glastonbury asking for help. The young monk volunteered to pit himself against the forces of evil and rode to Wookey Hole with the Abbot's blessing,

◀The Witch of Wookey?

carrying a wooden cross and a phial of holy water. As he ventured inside the cave, the witch stepped forward, her eyes blazing.

'How dare you enter my dwelling?' she snarled. 'Do you not realise my great powers? I have destroyed your paltry marriage as I would snap a twig and I can destroy you just as easily.'

The monk watched her steadily and murmured prayers under his breath. The witch stirred up her pot and spoke a series of incantations over it until dark spirits appeared within the cave.

'There', she said proudly, 'I can call up spirits of evil to obey my commands. You achieve nothing with your psalms and your fruitless existence. Where is the young wife you loved so much? All your religion couldn't bring her back.'

At this the young monk reached for his phial and tossed the holy water in the witch's face. She uttered a terrible scream and the evil spirits vanished. In an instant she was turned to stone. Today her misshapen form still stands in the Great Cave, a grotesque

The grotesque stalactite known as the Witch of Wookey terrifies children who visit the caverns.

stalactite known as the Witch of Wookey which terrifies any children who visit the caverns.

Until this century, most people had assumed that this tale was simply a legend to explain the weird shape which the stalactite had formed over thousands of years. However, in 1912, excavations in the cave revealed the skeleton of a Romano-British woman lying beside a dagger and a white ball-like stalagmite usually called a witch-ball, so it seems there may have been more than a grain of truth in the legend.

The dig also revealed the remains of two goats who doubtless supplied the woman with milk and perhaps acted as her familiars. Whatever the truth, the discovery provides fascinating evidence of the way legend is created; the miserable existence of one eccentric old woman, transformed into a triumph for Christianity.

St Aloys

Another such triumph would have made any RSPCA inspector literally hopping mad if he had arrived during the miracle. St Aloys was a holy man who lived at Wincanton. He was famous for his gift of casting out evil spirits and for his deep empathy with animals, particularly horses. He was always asked to use his powers if any animal seemed to be past saving—and invariably succeeded, sometimes in extraordinary circumstances.

A carter who lived nearby had a fine horse which he loved dearly. The horse willingly carted stones each day to bring in a meagre living for his master, so it was a major tragedy when the strong hooves began to splinter through overwork. A great sand-crack appeared, as wide as a man's thumb, splitting the hoof from top to bottom.

The carter was heart-broken for not only had he lost his livelihood but he believed his horse would have to be destroyed. The blacksmith too was at his wits' end, particularly when the crack became infected and the horse could hardly bear to put his foot to the ground. As the hoof grew more and more inflamed, the Devil entered the horse through the crack and the maddened creature lashed out at anyone who came near. His eyes lost their old mildness and rolled madly while anyone who tried to stroke the drenched and shaking neck risked a vicious bite.

An alabaster plaque tells the story of St Aloys healing the horse.

The blacksmith despaired and sent for the butcher but when the carter caught sight of the cruel axe, he knew he must do something to try to save his horse from that fate. He sent a message to St Aloys, begging him for help. The Saint arrived at once but by now the horse seemed utterly possessed, thrown from side to side of the stable by unseen hands and whinnying uncontrollably in a demonic frenzy.

'I'm afraid he's past all help,' said the carter sadly. 'Try if you like, but you'll never get him to stand.'

'Don't you worry about that,' the Saint assured him. 'He'll stand all right. The good Lord has more power than a cartload of devils.'

The Saint ran his hand slowly up the red-hot flank and disappeared outside, carrying something under his arm. When the carter glanced at his horse, he could hardly believe his eyes. The Devil had left him and he stood quietly on three legs, whickering into his hay, while next door in the smithy, St Aloys began to shoe the detached leg. Miraculously the great sand-crack was healed and after tapping the last nails into the shoe, the Saint bustled back into the stable.

'Here we are then,' he announced in businesslike fashion and clapped the leg back on in an instant. He behaved utterly as if this were the normal way of shoeing a horse. Together he and the carter knelt in the stable to give thanks for the last-ditch miracle. The horse now stood calmly with no sign that his leg had ever been removed. From that day on, his coat gleamed like a conker, his hooves shone like black silk and he continued carting stones for many a long year.

This delightful story is commemorated with great gusto in an alabaster plaque in Nottingham Castle Museum. This exhibit is a relief carving taken from an altar piece and shows 'Saint Eloi shoeing a horse possessed of the Devil'.

These days, the attitude of most celebrities is 'I don't mind what they say about me so long as they spell my name right'. St Aloys had no such vanity but, despite the variations on his name, his fame spread and he doubtless put the local vets out of business.

Bladud, King and Swineherd

The life of Bladud, one of the earliest kings of Britain was also deeply bound up with animals, though very much against his will for he went from the luxury of a royal court to the squalor of herding swine, and back to luxury again. As a young man in the eighth century BC he seemed to have a golden future assured. He was the eldest son of Lud Hudibras, the 8th King of Britain and a direct descendant of Brutus, the founder of the dynasty. He was highly intelligent, handsome and talented but despite all this, modest and charming.

Everyone at his father's court near Stonehenge was devastated when the dreaded white spot of leprosy appeared on his hand. At first his father hid him away in a secret room at the palace but the news leaked out. Terrified of an epidemic King Lud's subjects petitioned for Bladud to be sent away and with heavy hearts his parents agreed. They could not even kiss him for fear of infection but as his weeping mother said her farewells from a safe distance, she rolled a fine, intricately chased ring towards him.

'Keep this ring with you always', she commanded 'and if you are ever restored to health, this will prove to me who you are.'

Bladud took the ring and threaded it onto a fine gold chain round his neck then wandered away with his life in ruins. He slept rough and lived on berries and nuts, keeping well away from the sight of men in the dense oak forests that covered the west of England.

At last hunger drove him to look for work and he camouflaged his sores with mud. An old swineherd at what is now Keynsham took pity on him and gave him the lowliest job of all, as a swineherd's boy, driving the herd from pasture to pasture. The herd of pigs flourished and grew fat on the carpet of acorns until to his horror, they caught his dreaded disease and became as scaly and leprous as himself. He dared not go back to the old swineherd but drove the herd ever further to hide his shame. At a spot where the River Avon ran shallow and chattering across stones he saw on the far bank a real cornucopia of acorns. The pigs plunged and snorted to be allowed across so Bladud drove them through the river. The crossing is called Swineford to this day. Bladud set up camp among the trees and the place is now known as Upper Swainswick, sup-posedly from Swine's wick, though etymologists dispute this.

The next day, as he led the pigs out of their pens, they were seized with mass hysteria and maddened by the pain of their disease they rushed like Gadarene swine along the forest paths and down into the valley. Bladud followed as fast as he could but only found them hours later, rolling ecstatically in a warm swamp thick with rotting leaves and smooth bubbling slime. Conscientious as ever, Bladud washed them down and for once they didn't roll or scratch the bleeding sores on their sides. He examined them carefully, hardly daring to believe his eyes. Their scaly patches were beginning to fade and they already looked healthier.

Each day he let them wallow to their hearts' content and within a few weeks they were cured. He tried the same treatment on himself and at last he too walked from the warm springs without a mark on him. He reached for the ring his mother gave him years before, then drove the herd back to Keynsham. Somehow he persuaded the swineherd that his incredible story was true and the two set off for Hudibras's court. A feast was in progress and the retainers, seeing simply a filthy old swineherd and his ragged boy, wouldn't let them in so Bladud begged a servant to drop the ring into the queen's goblet. She drained the cup in the final toast and caught her breath as she saw the exquisite band of bright gold. She let out a cry.

'My child, Bladud. He is here. I must see him.' Bladud was ushered in and given place of honour as his parents wept for joy.

'To his horror the herd of pigs caught his dreaded disease and became as scaly and leprous as himself.'

He became once more heir apparent and spent several years in Greece, becoming a great scholar of mathematics, philosophy and necromancy. When he came to the throne eleven years later, he set up his court around the hot swamp that had cured his leprosy. Here he built his capital which he called Caer Badon, today the city of Bath and dedicated the springs to a goddess called Sul.

The Romans later named the place Aquae Sulis and called the great hill overlooking the city Solisbury. Even when his fortunes were restored, Bladud did not forget the old swineherd but set him up in style with many herds of swine in a place that soon came to be known as Hog's Norton.

Sadly for Bladud, his great classical learning and fascination with science eventually caused his downfall for he made a pair of wings and tried to fly from the temple which he built to Apollo on the summit of Solisbury Hill. Perhaps the gods wanted to punish him like Daedalus and Icarus for overweening arrogance for he soared

Looking down on Bath. 'Here he built his capital which he called Caer Badon, today the city of Bath.'

'Bladud Buildings is a row of Georgian houses in the Paragon . . .'

gracefully into the air then plummeted to his death. Although he is now hardly remembered outside Bath, he was succeeded by his son Lear whose story formed the basis of the Skakespearean tragedy.

Bladud's great achievements generated much envy and many rejected his account of how he chanced upon the warm muddy swamp. Because of his interest in necromancy, some claimed that Bladud actually created the hot springs by witchcraft. In one highly unscientific version, he is said to have buried four tuns in the earth below the city, two made of burning brass and two of glass filled with salt and brimstone. Once these were placed over the natural springs, they fermented and kept the water boiling as it bubbled up from the ground. The springs soon became famous for their healing properties.

In Bath, the King's name is still in evidence. Bladud Buildings is a row of Georgian houses in the Paragon overlooking the city while Bladud's statue is visible from the middle window of the Pump Room. The figure, complete with robes and crown is set into a niche behind the King's bath. An inscribed tablet below it reads:

61

Bladud, son to Lud Hudibras,
The Eighth King of the Britons
From Brute; a Great Philosopher
And Mathematician: bred at Athens
And Recorded the First Discoverer
And Founder of these Bathes, Eight
Hundred Sixty and Three yeares
Before Christ, that is Two Thousand
Five Hundred Thirty Five Years
SINCE
ANNO DOMINI 1672

This detailed information usually comes as a surprise to visitors who arrive convinced that the baths were founded by the Romans and although most people have heard of King Lear, few realise his father's role in the creation of the city.

The Battle of Sedgemoor

Nearer the present day, a King, who never was, has more than made his mark. The Protestant 'King' Monmouth staged his rebellion three hundred years ago and the legends surrounding that tragic action, far from dying out, are on the increase. Over the centuries and up to the present day, scores of sober people claim to have seen spectral figures fleeing from the battlefield or heard the hoofbeats and jingling harness of unseen soldiers. To the people living nearby, the protagonists—Monmouth, the Catholic King James II and, in the bloody aftermath, Judge Jeffreys—are as real as today's politicians. Every ancient tree or crossroads is said to be the site of a hanging or an unquiet grave.

In the uprising, James, Duke of Monmouth, the illegitimate son of Charles II pressed his claim to the throne. In 1685 he had himself proclaimed King at Taunton and gathered an army of several thousand men, most badly armed and with no experience of fighting. He also went on a so-called 'Royal Progress' round the Westcountry to enlist new recruits but, as fast as men joined up, others left to return to their families. Most of the gentry refused to join, although many had been friendly in earlier years and one had even witnessed miraculous proof of Monmouth's royalty.

BLADUD SON OF LUDHUDIBRAS
EIGHTH KING OF THE BRITANS,
FROM BRUTE A GREAT PHILOSOPH
& MATHEMATICIAN, BRED AT
ATHENS & RECORDED THE FIRST
DISCOVERER AND FOUNDER OF
THESE BATHS EIGHT HUNDRED
SIXTY THREE YEARS BEFORE
CHRIST, THAT IS TWO THOUSAND
FIVE HUNDRED SIXTY TWO YEAR
TO THE PRESENT YEAR 1699

Statue of Bladud is set into a niche behind the King's bath.

In 1680, Sir John Paulett of Hinton St George was feasting Monmouth and his friends beneath the great trees in the rolling parkland of Hinton House. It was an idyllic scene and Monmouth must have thought that on Charles II's death, nothing could stand between him and the throne. As the handsome young Duke laughed and drank, a young girl limped into the park unnoticed, one eye and half her face disfigured with a great running sore. She was a widow's daughter from Crewkerne, desperately ill with scrofula, a tubercular disease also known as the King's Evil.

Traditionally this could only be cured by touching a king or his garment. Doctors had already despaired of the girl's life and as she trudged the three miles from Crewkerne to Hinton St George, she knew this was her last chance. Her face lit up as she saw the languid figure holding court in the shade and she crept closer to the table.

'God bless your greatness,' she whispered, clutching his wrist. The Duke started back as he noticed the scabs on her body but kept his composure.

'God bless you my girl,' he smiled. She melted away into the crowd but a few days later came the news that she was completely cured with only a few small scars left as evidence.

The miracle later gave weight to Monmouth's claims to the throne. He was further encouraged by a gipsy fortune-teller's warning to beware of the rhine. He assumed she meant the River Rhine and since he had no intention of transferring hostilities to the continent, he thought he had nothing to fear. It was to prove a costly mistake.

Once James II heard of the rising, he ordered his army to march down to the Westcountry to crush it. They camped just outside the village of Weston Zoyland on the flat Sedgemoor Plain, once marsh but by then drained with huge ditches. On one side the Royalists were defended by the broad water-filled channel known as Bussex Rhyne.

Monmouth's army attacked, hoping to take the Royalists by surprise, but the deep rhine held up their advance and gave King James's men the chance to grab their arms and group for battle. Better armed and equipped and all trained soldiers, they made short work of the rebels. Soon the battlefield was littered with dead and dying men while the more fortunate fled pell-mell into the surrounding countryside. The gipsy's prophecy had been fatally fulfilled.

Even now, on clear nights, most often in the small hours of 6 July, people claim they have heard the sounds of battle and the disembodied voices of escaping rebels shouting 'Come over' as they urge their comrades to safety. Some say they have seen Monmouth himself and one of his officers, Lord Grey, galloping flat out over the moor, their horses' hooves pounding the moist black soil.

In 1850 a great circular gravemound came to light as the earth subsided below the moorland surface. Eighty years later a more conventional memorial was erected. A woman from Chedzoy, Elizabeth Winter, was weeping uncontrollably one night because her collie dog had been injured and destroyed. In the midst of her grief she heard an unearthly voice which said:

'You weep for your dog. What of my poor lambs, lying unmourned and unremembered in your fields?' Inspired by the message, she

She was desperately ill with scrofula— the King's Evil. ▶

organised a public subscription for a monument and in 1928 a slab
of Cornish granite was raised, bearing the words:

To the Glory of God
And in Memory of All Those Who
Doing the Right as they Gave it
Fell in the Battle of Sedgemoor
6th July 1685
And Lie Buried in this Field
or Who for their Share in the Fight
Suffered Death
Punishment or Transportation
Pro Patria.

Today the slab is flanked by four smaller memorials, mushroom-
like staddle stones. Each bears the names of famous battles fought
in one of the past four centuries.

To find the monument, turn left off the A372 from Bridgwater
along Penzoy Drove, the last track before the outskirts of Weston
Zoyland. After a quarter of a mile, another track, Zog Drove,
branches right then turns first left. The stone is on the left set in a
small enclosure. Bussex Rhyne is now a wide, dry channel running
across land to the right of Zog Drove.

I visited the spot in early autumn, a faint haze over the flat plain.
The landscape has probably changed little since 1685 and most of
the drainage ditches and dykes mentioned by historians are still
visible. All the same, apart from the stone with its simple, moving
inscription, that counterpane of fertile fields shows no outward sign
of the bloody drama once enacted there. The land seems almost
featureless and indistinguishable from a thousand other level tracts
of Somerset earth. It is only by looking at engravings of the time
and reading eyewitness accounts of the battle that the whole
conflict comes to life in the mind's eye. Then, the bare dates and
'facts' of the school history books are transmuted into shouts, panic
and desperate struggle and the reason for so many sightings and
inexplicable phenomena becomes clear.

Many such sightings have spanned the centuries. In 1924 a
London journalist was driving along a lonely road near Sedgemoor
when he saw ahead a man dressed in old-fashioned clothes and
riding a great grey horse. The man looked straight ahead and
ignored the driver's greeting. Although the horse was cantering

Sedgemoor Memorial Stone.

down the road, there was no sound of hooves. The hairs rose on the journalist's neck and as he watched, the couple jumped a small obstacle where none was visible then melted into the mist. Shivering, he drove to the village and told the locals what he had seen. His description tallied exactly with contemporary accounts of Monmouth's flight from the battlefield.

The first legends of the doomed rebellion sprang up at once and in many Monmouth retained his regal qualities. It is said that when his horse flagged, he was given a fresh mount and temporary shelter in the village of Chedzoy leaving behind a silver lover's buckle which later cured the King's Evil.

Although Monmouth was found cowering in a ditch and beheaded on Tower Hill, many still longed to see King James overthrown and created myths to keep their hopes alive. As with Sir Francis Drake and King Arthur, some clutched at the belief that their hero was not dead but in exile and would come again to lead them to victory. A certain faction believed that one of Monmouth's followers who strongly resembled him had sacrificed himself on the block, allowing his leader to escape to Holland. The Duke soon attained the status of folk hero and a century after the uprising, some Somerset miners still believed that he was alive and would return to right their wrongs.

Hanging Judge Jeffreys and the Persecution

The retribution which followed the rebellion left a still deeper mark on folk-memory and provides a rich store of legends. James decided to make an example of the rebels *'pour encourager les autres'* and sent the Lord Chief Justice, Judge Jeffreys, to try those captured after the battle. Although he was an able lawyer, he was hated and feared for his natural streak of violence, aggravated by an agonising bladder stone. True, he sincerely believed that to fight on Monmouth's side constituted High Treason but even those loyal to the King disliked his fierce language and bullying tactics.

He went from centre to centre, trying the rebels in batches with an executioner in tow. In the end about 200 were hanged and 1,000 others transported to the colonies as slaves. Many of those hanged do not rest peacefully in their graves.

Heddon Oak

The Heddon Oak which stood until recently on the Crowcombe to Stogumber road was well-known as a Hanging Tree. Here the mutilated bodies of six of Monmouth's followers, three from each village, were hung up as a dreadful warning to other would-be rebels. Afterwards, many people claimed they heard spectral groans and the rattling of chains as they passed the ancient tree. The quietest horse would shy uncontrollably for no apparent reason and sometimes galloping hooves thundered up behind solitary travellers although no horse ever materialised.

Despite its historic associations, the oak was cut down amid some controversy in 1979 because it was rotten. Even now the spot where it stood still possesses a curious atmosphere, half-melancholy, half-sinister and I never pass it at nightfall without looking over my shoulder.

The Hanging Boy

Judge Jeffreys seemed to relish making an example of the rebels. One man however took his revenge in a manner that reeked of witch-craft. The only son of a farmer from Walton near Street went to fight for the rebel cause and was captured after the battle. His father was desperate to save him from the gallows. He sold the whole of that year's harvest and spent his life-savings trying to secure a pardon, but the Judge was adamant. The boy must hang, and in full view of his father at Marshall's Elm near the farm.

Throughout the grim ritual, the farmer stood stony-faced, his eyes like dead coals, but when it was all over and the pathetic figure swung gently beneath the boughs, the farmer uttered one cry and strode into the stables. He slaughtered his best bullock, ripped out the great bleeding heart, then beat a score of nails through it. Next he placed it in the chimney where it scorched and smoked for years.

From that day on, the Judge suffered a series of choking attacks when his whole heart seemed transfixed by searing pains and he fought for breath. At those times, a haunting image rose before his eyes, whether he closed them or not, the sight of the hanging boy.

Mary Bridge

The Royalist soldiers did not restrict their attention to the rebels themselves. Their womenfolk too were unofficially considered fair game, although Colonel Kirke refuted this during an extraordinary trial at Taunton.

Mary Bridge was a twelve-year-old girl who lived at Weston Court in Weston Zoyland. Her parents were on the side of the rebels and after the battle, a troop of the King's men called at her home to question them. During their visit, one of the soldiers made an insult-ing suggestion to Mary's mother. She answered him defiantly and the man started to use force. Mary snatched up a sword and stabbed him to the heart.

Although she was summoned to a court-martial under Colonel Kirke in Taunton, she was honourably acquitted and presented with the sword which was handed down through the family for three centuries. It is now on show in Taunton Museum, a small dress sword

about two feet long with a basket handle and a blunt tip that makes you wonder how it ever killed anyone.

Betrayed by a Spaniel

The officers in Monmouth's army were the prime targets of King James's vengeance and he mercilessly hounded even those who managed to escape after the battle. Locking Manor near Weston-super-Mare is the site of just such a persecution, although its owner might well have survived had it not been for a frightened white spaniel.

John Plomley was the local squire and he and his two sons fought for Monmouth's cause. Both youths were captured; one was hanged, the other imprisoned, but John, a high-ranking officer in Monmouth's army, escaped and hid in the Cheddar caves for several weeks until he thought the coast was clear.

Once the hue and cry had died down, he disguised himself and made his way home to his grieving wife but Royalist spies were everywhere and a party of soldiers came to search the Manor. Plomley saw them coming and hid in a secret passage behind the panelling. The soldiers pushed past his wife and searched the great house from top to bottom without success. Lady Plomley watched them in silence, her white spaniel in her arms but as the grim-faced men turned to go, the dog wriggled out of her clutches. He sped down the corridor to the room where Plomley was hiding and barked madly at the patch of panelling that concealed the secret passage.

The soldiers followed him, convinced he would lead them to his master. They began tapping each square of panelling until they found the hollow one, then eased it aside on its rollers. Plomley heard the commotion and dashed along the passage which led to the outbuildings of Locking Head farm three quarters of a mile away. Here he emerged and sought shelter in a small coppice but the King's men followed close behind and soon captured him.

The inevitable penalty was death and his wife was brought to see him hanged, drawn and quartered. She arrayed herself in her finest

◀'He barked madly at the patch of panelling that concealed the secret passage.'

clothes and put on the Plomley jewels, standing proudly until the dreadful deed was done. Then she broke down and wept. Frenzied with grief, she rushed back to Locking Manor and snatching up the little white spaniel who had led the soldiers to her husband, she threw herself headlong into the well.

The manor's present owner, Lloyd Walters, has seen her ghost three times, once at the far end of a passage, a misty figure in a pointed hat with a frill and a long cloak. Others say they have seen the apparition gliding swiftly through the garden with a white dog in her arms. She usually disappears near the well.

In the early sixties a cleaner working upstairs shrieked violently and rushed from the house. Although she knew nothing of the legend, she had seen the shadowy form of a white spaniel in the room and she never set foot in the house again. The manor has been made into four flats but it remains a square, imposing, black-and-white house in the centre of the village. After the discovery of a skeleton behind the panelling in the thirties, the secret passage was sealed off at either end and now only the top two steps of it are visible.

The original well was discovered twenty years ago during excavations at the back of the house when a slab was unearthed over a full column of water about forty feet deep. The present owners believe there may be a ledge and possible passageway three quarters of the way down but neither Lady Plomley's skeleton nor the jewels have ever been found.

The Champion Runner Of Sedgemoor

Another heartbroken woman whose lover suffered the same fate as John Plomley likewise haunts the spot where he died. Samuel Sweet was the champion runner of Sedgemoor and like many of his comrades fought bravely in Monmouth's army but was captured and dragged before Lord Feversham who summarily hanged many of the rebels.

Feversham was a betting man and when he heard of Sweet's

'She waves her white arms above her head and shakes her flowing hair in a frenzy of grief.'▶

prowess as a runner, he promised him his life and freedom if he could keep pace with his best horse galloping flat out. The young man's sweetheart had come to plead for her lover's life and she rejoiced when she heard of the wager for she believed he could outrun even the fleetest horse.

In another account, Sweet was roped naked to a wild moorland colt for the vital race but whatever the equine competition the young man flew like the wind over a three-quarter mile stretch towards Brentsfield Bridge, beating the horse by a length. He collapsed, feet bleeding and sides heaving at the superhuman effort of the run but when he appealed to Lord Feversham for his freedom, the officer dismissed the bet entirely.

'It was laid merely in jest, you Somerset cur. We do not bargain with traitors.' The soldiers laughed derisively and strung him up from the nearest tree, deaf to his sweetheart's prayers and tears. The girl wept hysterically as her lover's life ebbed away then at the barbaric sight of his butchered remains, she went mad and later died of grief.

Even now on misty nights, her ghost is sometimes seen, moaning round the site of the great grave mound. She waves her white arms above her head and shakes her flowing hair in a frenzy of grief.

The Cornish poet, Charles Causley, tells the tragic story most strikingly in his dramatic ballad 'The Song of Samuel Sweet'. First Lord Feversham wagers the rebel his life:

> 'Cut him down, troopers,
> From the forest skies,
> Breakaway the bandage
> That binds his clear eyes.
> Let him go a-coursing
> My charger and me!
> If he be the victor,
> He shall go free!

After the race, Samuel Sweet is bewildered at the troopers' response:

> 'O Captain, I am waiting
> By the empty tree
> As your horse of fire
> Comes blazing on the lea.

74

See, my feet are bloody,
With salt my eyes are blind
For Captain, I have left you
Far, far behind.

'Why do you frown, Captain,
As I bend the knee,
Nor tell your tossing troopers
That I may go free?
Why do you tie my collar
With a shining strand,
Nor send me home to mother,
A ring-dove in my hand?

Swayne's Leaps

A few rebels, however, did manage to escape with their lives and
one, likewise a noted athlete, made his getaway through a clever
trick. Jan Swayne was the champion jumper of the district and he,
too, fought on Monmouth's side. Although he escaped after the
Battle of Sedgemoor and made his way home, he was recaptured
and dragged from his bed as he slept. The troopers bound his hands
and marched him along the road to Bridgwater with his weeping
wife and children trailing along behind.

Swayne kept his wits about him and as they passed Loxley
Woods, exercised the condemned man's prerogative. He begged to
be allowed to show his children his prodigious leaps for the last
time. The officer stupidly agreed and commanded the troopers to
release him. Jan Swayne seized his chance and threw himself
through the thicket in four great bounds. Reaching a little stream
running down through the wood and heavily overhung with bushes,
he dashed up it, bent double and disappeared leaving the astounded
troopers groping vainly through the boggy undergrowth.

They searched all day, cursing Jan Swayne for his cunning but
marvelling at the length of his leaps. They never saw him again and
even missed the chance to take his family hostage for by the time
they had gathered their senses, his wife and children had melted
away into the bracken as if by magic.

One of the stones (right) marking Swayne's leaps where he threw himself through the thicket in four great bounds (far right).

The local people set up a row of stones to show the length of the jumps and commemorate the great feat. They are still known as Swayne's leaps and lie in the marshy woodland a few yards off the Glastonbury to Bridgwater Road. Although a faded board nailed to an oak tree marks their position, they are almost impossible to find as they are no bigger than large fists and half covered with leaves and bracken.

I was lucky enough to meet a local farmer, one of the few who knew how to find them. He obligingly plunged through holly bush, briar and bog until a little energetic scrambling revealed them lying in a straight line about fourteen feet apart. The end stone was placed just beside a brackish stream, the one where Swayne made his audacious escape. As the grey humps like miniature tombstones appeared from under the dead leaves, I felt a real thrill of exploration and discovery that made all the scratches and muddy boots worthwhile. The stones' very obscurity added to the excitement and suddenly Jan Swayne himself and the swaggering troopers seemed very near. I tried to jump the distance between two of the stones

and even with a good run-up, failed miserably. All the same, I could sense how Swayne must have felt as he leapt for his life, bounding as he always did at the local fairs and races, but with more at stake than ever before. Suddenly my ungainly jump became a triumphant leap back in time three hundred years.

To find the stones, take the A39 road from Glastonbury towards Bridgwater. 300 yards beyond the first driveway on the left as you pass through Loxley Woods, turn left into the wood. The stones lie along a narrow track running parallel to the road about twenty yards from it. Good hunting!

Walford's Gibbet and Dead Woman's Ditch

A spot marked like Swayne's Leaps on the Ordnance Survey maps but far easier to find is the site of Walford's Gibbet. This was the final scene of a tragic drama caused by one man's frustration and

Walford's Gibbet: ' . . . hanged near the site of his crime.'

society's rigid refusal to tolerate weakness. Walford was a charcoal burner in the 1780s who plied his lonely trade in the oak scrub on the Quantocks above Nether Stowey. He was none too bright and when a half-witted girl called night after night at his hut and sat there, simpering dumbly, he followed his instincts with no idea of the possible consequences.

Inevitably she became pregnant and a local scandal erupted. Although Walford had been betrothed to a beautiful young woman, the overseer of the parish forced him to wed the idiot-girl. The shotgun marriage never prospered and turned to an agonising war of attrition. Walford's black rages became more violent and uncontrollable and his wife degenerated into a cunning shrew, sniggering darkly to herself in corners or taunting him with what he had lost.

One night after the two had been drinking heavily at the Castle of Comfort, the old alehouse in Nether Stowey, they staggered out, Walford morose and silent, his wife giggling inanely. As they began the long trudge back to their hut, Walford sank deeper into his black dog mood and his wife began her endless jibes.

'A fine girl she was—hair as yaller as gold. Got me instead though, didn't you—a fine bargain, me and the babby—your babby!' and she threw back her head and cackled. Walford spun round in a fury and something snapped within him. Grasping the woman's throat he squeezed tighter and tighter then shook her as a dog shakes vermin; shook and shook until the cackling gave way to sobbing gasps and at length the gasps ceased entirely. He glanced behind him. The road was empty so he flung the limp figure across his shoulders and half-ran, keeping to the shadows until he reached a lonely ditch on the crown of the Quantocks. Here he shovelled out a shallow grave, scooping up the earth frantically with a flat stone and lowered in the corpse. The livid face glimmered in the dark, the lips drawn back as if in a snarl.

Desperate to hide all evidence of his crime, Walford piled up dead leaves above the mound and slunk home to his hut, trembling and almost incoherent with rage.

'She made me do it. She led me on,' he sobbed to himself, 'but I got the better of her.'

He was wrong, for within a few days, the girl's father, himself a charcoal burner, noticed her disappearance and became suspicious. Walford's contempt for his wife was well-known and soon search parties were out scouring the hills. When they found the pathetic form in the ditch, the guilt pointed only one way. Walford was arrested and condemned to death at Bridgwater Assizes.

As was the custom, he was brought back in a waggon to be hanged near the site of his crime. The horses strained as they drew the cart slowly up the hill and Walford passed the familiar scenes of his childhood with an unseeing stare, his chains clanking about his neck. Soon he was swinging lifeless from the great gibbet.

His executioners hung his body in chains and left it as a dire warning to passers-by. The gibbet remained there until early in the nineteenth century when it was sawn in half and made into two gateposts. Even then, many people claimed that on windy nights they could still hear the rattling of spectral chains and glimpse the shadow of a hanging man.

Today the site of the gibbet is simply a grassy verge to the left of the coach road to Crowcombe, three hundred yards above the village of Nether Stowey where the road bears sharply to the right. A mile or so on towards Crowcombe, amid rolling Quantock moorland is the spot where Walford hid his wife's body. It is now a flat square of ground beside the road, surrounded by grassy banks on three sides and flanked by a hedge. The Quantock Stag Hounds often meet there and the quiet, almost melancholy place is famous throughout Somerset as Dead Woman's Ditch.

Cadbury Castle

Cadbury Castle is a fortress fit for a king—King Arthur in legend and perhaps in fact. Even today it looks the part, imposing in its size and position, inaccessible and well-defended by the steep, rocky ramparts and by the four concentric fosses, banks and trenches which snake round the hillside to impede the enemy.

It was certainly the stronghold of a Dark Age chieftain in the sixth century about the time the real Arthur was harrying the Saxon invaders in a series of fierce battles. Excavations in 1966 unearthed further evidence suggesting this might have been Arthur's headquarters. Many male skeletons were found packed into trenches in the field called Westwoods, west of the camp. Those who discovered them were convinced that these were Arthur's warriors buried after the last and bloodiest battle.

The name of the nearby River Camel likewise fuelled speculation

'Cadbury Castle is a fortress fit for a king.'

that this was in fact Camelot, although the first mention of this came in the sixteenth century when Leland wrote:

'At the very South Ende of the Church of South Cadbyri standithe Camalotte, sumtyme a famose Town or Castell. Much Gold, Sylver and Coper of the Romaine Coynes hathe been found there yn plowing; and lykewise in the fields, in the rootes of this Hille, with many other antique things and especial by Eeste.

'Ther was found in hominum memorium a Horse Shoe of Sylver at Camallotte. The people can tell nothing ther, but they have herd say that Arture much resortid to Camalat.'

If this really was Arthur's court, it would have been a world away from the glittering, fairytale Camelot of the Medieval romances and the chivalric ideal of Tennyson's *Idylls of the King* and Malory's *Morte d'Arthur;* no plumes or knights in armour and cloth of gold or any of the Gothic splendours of the courtly tales of love and battle.

The real Arthur would have been an early guerrilla fighter, using the tactics of speed and surprise to keep the Saxons under pressure, his Camelot a bleak, windswept fortress, military camp rather than castle, the lives of his men almost certainly 'nasty, brutish and short'.

Whatever the realities, the Westcountry people desperately

81

needed to believe in a great and glorious leader who would right their wrongs and restore their fortunes. Arthur fitted the bill and gradually acquired the trappings of later ages and the whole legendary mantle of supernatural powers, even immortality itself. There are hundreds of stories, many set in Somerset, that keep alive the image of Arthur as hero and saviour.

In one legend, Cadbury is hollow and King Arthur and his knights sleep inside the great cavern, waiting for the day when they will awake and save England. Some say that every seven years, a secret door opens in the hillside and the King and his men ride out and gallop round the ramparts, then set off along King Arthur's Hunting Causeway which runs from between the North and South Barrows, towards Glastonbury. Before the land was drained, this was a raised way through the marshes. It was used as a bridlepath until the early years of this century but it is now scarcely visible.

Arthur's Well on the fourth fosse of the fort's eastern slope is credited with magical powers. A true-hearted person who bathes his eyes in it on St John's Eve is said to be able to see the King and his

Arthur's Well at Cadbury
(far left) is credited with
magical powers.

men in their tranced sleep within the hollow hill and to glimpse
them as they gallop along the ancient track, their hounds giving
tongue after stopping to drink at the well. To the rest of us they
must remain invisible except for a flash of silver horseshoes and a
jingling of bridles.

The Giants of Brent Knoll

Arthur is associated with many parts of Somerset and most of the
stories tell of his valour in battle and his betrayal by the evil
Mordred and the faithless Queen Guinevere. The loyalty of his own
followers remained constant and when he set a young man a
herculean task, it was accomplished against all odds. The tragic
outcome haunted Arthur for the rest of his life.

Brent Knoll is the steep mound rising out of the central Somerset
plain beside the M5. Its Roman name was Mons Ranarum, mount of
frogs, an appropriate description for it was then a great green

citadel rearing up out of a tract of flooded marsh, with only a single reed-strewn causeway leading to and from it.

At the time of Arthur, three fierce giants occupied the fortress and murdered all travellers that crossed the causeway. King Arthur was spending the Feast of the Nativity at Caerleon and at the height of the festivities he knighted a brave young prince called Ider who begged to be given some difficult task to prove his prowess. Arthur was bound for Glastonbury and he sent him on ahead to do battle with the giants. The young man accepted the dread task fearlessly and set off, desperate to show himself worthy of his new rank.

As the King and his troop approached Brent Knoll, they heard fearful sounds of combat and broke into a gallop. They were too late. The mound was flowing with blood and the slight figure of Ider lay dead beside the massive corpses of the three giants. Arthur was filled with remorse and bore the young man's body in state to

Brent Knoll: ' . . . three fierce giants occupied the fortress and murdered all who crossed the causeway.'

Glastonbury. Here he ordered the monks to say masses for his soul and in memory of Ider's great feat, gave Brent Knoll and the lands of Brent Marsh to the monastery, as well as a wonderful, bejewelled chalice, the richest he possessed.

For centuries, the tale was considered pure fiction but in the 1880s an ancient cuirass of heavy Roman craftsmanship dug up near East Brent added weight to the legend.

Glastonbury, Isle of Avalon

It was not pure chance that led King Arthur and his men the winding way through the marshes to Glastonbury. The mysterious island, floating upon the fens, with its steep and unmistakable Tor silhouetted against the Somerset sky was a great religious centre and even then a place of pilgrimage. No wonder so many believe this was Avalon, the Isle of Apples, where Arthur came, mortally wounded after the last battle.

In many of the stories the aging King made his final heroic stand on the banks of the crooked River Camel in the famous battle of Camlann. Here Mordred, Arthur's bastard son, dealt his father the fatal blow, a wound that was found etched on his skull centuries later. The stricken leader was secretly carried to Glastonbury across the nine feet wide Roman causeway, uncovered in the nineteenth century. It was built of alder branches and oak piles and paved with stone. On the outskirts of the town, the darkened procession crossed the River Brue near the present day bridge of Pomparles—from *pons perilis*. Although the Brue is now just a trickle, it was far more *'perilis'* then and formed a wide mere for most of the year.

This was perhaps where Arthur flung his great sword Excalibur, returning it to the Lady of the Lake whose arm, 'clothed in white samite, mystic, wonderful' rose from the broad surface, caught the glittering weapon and vanished without a ripple. Many claim that on misty nights they have seen a man with a dreadful head wound stagger into the centre of the bridge and whirl a massive sword into the Brue.

Accounts of Arthur's end differ. In several, including Tennyson's, he was rowed across the shallow mere by three queens in a barge, 'dark as a funeral scarf from stem to stern', to the mystical Isle of Avalon to be healed.

**King Arthur, mortally wounded, was rowed in a barge
to the Isle of Avalon.**

Geoffrey of Monmouth, a historian not averse to a little myth-making of his own wrote: 'The renowned King Arthur was wounded deadly and was borne thence unto the island of Avalon for the healing of his wounds, where he gave up the crown unto his kinsman Constantine, son of Cador in A.D. 542.'

Most people, however, believe he was carried to the Celtic Abbey near the site of the present Lady Chapel and was buried in the hollowed out trunk of an oak tree between two pyramids or pillars. His wife Guinevere became an abbess and when she died was taken from her convent at Amesbury and laid to rest beside him. On dark nights, many have seen the spectral flickerings of the torches that lit her bier moving along the road from Shepton Mallet to Glastonbury.

The great coffin was placed deep in the ground beneath a stone slab with a small cross of Mendip lead and an inscription facing inwards to hide the King's identity. Although some, like Malory in his *Morte d'Arthur*, claim this read 'Hic jacet Arthurus, rex

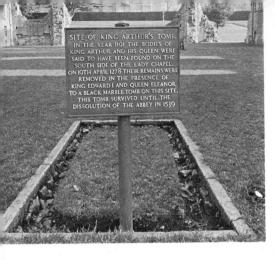

The site of
King Arthur's black
marble tomb in the ruins
of Glastonbury Abbey (far left).

quondam rexque futurus' (Here lies Arthur, the once and future king), more reliable accounts render it as 'Hic jacet sepultus inclytus Rex Arthurus in insula Avonia' (Here lies buried the illustrious King Arthur in the Isle of Avalon).

In the poignant difference between the two versions, the one full of yearning for future glories, the other a bald statement of fact, lie all the hopes of a people desperately seeking a Christ-like warrior who would return to transform their lives and lead them triumphantly into eternity.

In 1190, during the reign of Henry II the monks excavated between the two pyramids on the south side of the abbey cemetery and uncovered Arthur's tomb. When they opened the oak coffin, they discovered the skeletons of a huge man and beside him a slender woman. A plait of golden hair, preserved for six centuries lay there but when a monk grasped it, the locks crumbled to dust in his fingers. Gerald of Wales watched the exhumation and recorded the sheer size of the King:

'The thigh bone when placed next to the tallest man present, as the abbot showed us and fastened to the ground by his foot, reached three inches above his knee.'

The discovery certainly came at a convenient time for the monks and for Henry II. The King, who now controlled Britain and much of France and Ireland, needed a great, unifying myth to bind the scattered peoples together. The monks needed money and prestige, for a disastrous fire six years earlier had destroyed much of the abbey and if Glastonbury could attract more pilgrims, the sale of relics and indulgences would bring in the revenue for the rebuilding.

Nearly a century later, the royal remains were moved to a position

89

of high honour in the great abbey and people flocked to the tomb. Nothing is now left of it and on the grass within the graceful skeleton of walls and arches which remains of the abbey today, an inscription reads:

'In the year 1191, the bodies of King Arthur and his queen were said to have been found on the south side of the Lady Chapel. On 19th April, 1278, their remains were removed in the presence of King Edward I and Queen Eleanor to a black marble tomb on this site. The tomb survived until the dissolution of the abbey in 1539.'

Although much of the abbey is now in ruins, its atmosphere of cloistered peace makes it a fitting resting place for a king. Looking up at the exquisite broken arch above what was once the west door, I reflected that this somehow symbolised both the past splendours of Arthur's reign and its incompleteness, for will he not return in time of need to save Britain?

Whether King Arthur is in fact dead or just sleeping, whether he was simply boosted as a convenient device to exalt Church and State and whether he really visited even a quarter of the places connected with him is immaterial. What matters is that he lives on in the minds of thousands of Westcountry people and will awaken, not only within the hollow hills but in the imagination of all who are captivated by the glittering myth of the once and future King.

King Arthur at Beckery

In all the legends, Arthur is described as both valiant and devout and in one extraordinary yet beautiful story he is physically linked with the Christ-child in a way that hints at his own immortality. Arthur was lodging at St Peter's convent, high on Wearyall Hill in Glastonbury for a period of prayer and penance when an angel appeared to him in a dream, commanding him to go to the hermitage of St Mary Magdalen on Beckery Knoll a little way west of Glastonbury. It was a place of pilgrimage as St Bridget had lived there but Arthur at first dismissed the dream as mere fantasy.

It was only when he had the identical experience three nights

◄Beckery Village: 'An angel appeared to Arthur
in a dream commanding him to go to Beckery Knoll.'

Mystery window at Beckery.

running that he began to take notice and told a servant of the angel's command. The man sneaked out and went quietly across the marshes to Beckery. He crept into the seemingly deserted chapel and caught his breath at the sight of a man's body on a bier flanked by four tapers. Glimpsing the heavy gold candlesticks on the altar, he stole one and fled down the aisle, but a robed figure stepped from the shadows and stabbed him before he reached the door. Mortally wounded he staggered back to Glastonbury and sobbed out his story to the King with his dying breath.

Arthur was astounded and the next night went to the church himself after a day of fasting and meditation. He saw a priest preparing for Mass and knelt at the altar rail but, as he prayed, a great light filled the chapel. Mary and her child appeared at the altar, radiant in glory. Arthur was transfixed for the priest offered him not bread and wine but the body of Christ himself. At a sign from the Virgin, he consumed the Holy Child who reappeared miraculously whole on the altar.

As Arthur knelt in awe, Mary approached the rail and gave him a

Glastonbury—the earliest site of Christian worship in Britain. ▶

crystal cross before vanishing with the baby in her arms. It was obscure, stunning traditions like this which emphasised Arthur's sanctity and underlined the parallels with Christ himself.

Joseph of Arimathea comes to Glastonbury

Long before the time of Arthur, Glastonbury was sacred to the God of the Underworld, Gwyn-ap-Nudd, and was believed to be the pagan meeting place of the dead. This perhaps explains its later metamorphosis into the mystical Isle of Avalon.

Throughout the ages, its extraordinary shape, jutting dramatically out of the shimmering Somerset marshes must have seemed to the credulous local people strange and magical as if the whole island had been created by supernatural forces. No wonder it was thought, like Cadbury Castle, to be hollow, peopled by strange, unearthly spirits and best avoided after nightfall.

Its greatest significance, though, is as the earliest site of Christian worship in Britain and its connections with Joseph of Arimathea. Joseph was the secret follower of Christ and provided a sepulchre for his body on the day of the Crucifixion. He was a just and honourable man, rich, influential and a member of the Sanhedrin.

It was the apocryphal 'Acts of Pilate' which linked him with the Holy Grail, the cup Christ used at the Last Supper, but it was not until much later that his voyage to Glastonbury was mentioned. In 1120, William of Malmesbury made almost the first reference to this although there was perhaps a long oral tradition in the Dark Ages.

By Medieval times, however, the cult of Joseph was well established and fostered by the Glastonbury monks to enhance the prestige of their abbey. Most accounts agree that Joseph came to Britain in AD 63 with a band of eleven missionaries and was granted Twelve Hides of land at Glastonbury by the pagan King Arviragus. Here, at Gabriel's command, he built a church of twisted wattles and clay where the tiny community lived out austere lives devoted to prayer and praise.

The Holy Thorn on Wearyall Hill.▶

The Glastonbury Holy Thorn

Scores of delightful traditions have grown up around this early mission. As he arrived on the outskirts of the town, Joseph is said to have thrust his staff into the ground and sighed 'Now are we Weary, all'. The place is still known as Wearyall Hill. The staff, a dry hawthorn stick grown from a thorn in Christ's crown at the Crucifixion, miraculously took root and bloomed every year at Christmas time. A poem published in 1520 mentions three hawthorns 'that groweth in Werall' and 'do burge and bere green leaves as freshe as othere in May'. When the calendar was changed in 1752, the thorn kept to its old routine and duly flowered on the original Christmas Day which had become 5 January.

It was considered dangerous to tamper with it as a puritan who tried to cut it down found to his cost. James Howell recorded that the man 'was wel served for his blind zeale' for a thorn flew off and blinded him in one eye. One royalist wrote 'Nay that miraculous thorn of Glassenbury which was wont to celebrate the Festival of Christ's Nativity by putting forth its leaves and flowers, was cut in pieces by these militia men that it might no longer preach the birthday of their saviour.'

All the same, one of the thorn's two trunks survived another thirty years and descendants of the original flourish in and around Glastonbury; two in the Abbey grounds, one on the ridge of Wearyall Hill and one outside St John the Baptist's Church. Every year, just before Christmas, local schoolchildren sing carols in a simple ceremony around the tree and flowering sprigs are cut and sent to the Queen and Queen Mother. No matter that this variety of hawthorn blooms naturally in the midst of winter; it remains for believers a strange and lovely phenomenon.

The Beast's Thorn

In one legend, the thorn's sanctity was recognised, even by animals. A man made the short pilgrimage from Ilminster to Glastonbury

◄ One of the Holy Thorns in Glastonbury Abbey: '. . . descendants of the original flourish . . .'

and agreed to bring back a holy relic to bless the village. His neighbours were furious when he returned with a single thorn in his hand and scoffed when he claimed that this had come from Christ's crown and would bloom on Christmas Day. He planted it beside the road and the shoot grew with amazing speed.

On Christmas Eve, just before midnight, a tremendous clatter awoke the villagers and they threw up their windows in amazement. All the sheep and cattle had escaped from locked folds and bartons and were trotting along the road towards the thorn led by the rich farmer's master bullock. The villagers followed close behind. There in the moonlight stood the tree shining white with blossom, the pilgrim already kneeling beside it. The animals clustered round. On the stroke of midnight, the great bullock lowed aloud and knelt down on the frosty ground, his head bowed in reverence.

The other beasts knelt too and slowly and shamefacedly the villagers followed suit. By now they all realised that they were blessed with a Holy Thorn.

In Ruth Tongue's book *Somerset Folklore* she gives a delightful account gleaned from an old man who went out with some friends one Christmas Eve to see if the tale were true.

'Twas dark, couldn't see nothing at all. Proper black and we had no light, zee, and all to a zudden, there was breathings all round us zeemlike whichever way we turn. Thic lane were full of cattle and we just turn and run for it. No, we never zee no thorn blossom nor I wouldn't go now if I was asked. Vull of cows thic lane was.'

Thomas Hardy mentions the same tradition in a wonderful poem that describes the imaginative leap needed for true belief which he and so many long to make:

> If someone said on Christmas Eve
> 'Come; see the oxen kneel
> In the lonely barton by yonder combe
> Our childhood used to know,'
> I should go with him in the gloom,
> Hoping it might be so.

◄ The Beast's Thorn: 'On the stroke of midnight the great bullock lowed aloud and knelt down on the frosty ground his head bowed in reverence.'

**Generations of pilgrims
have tramped to Glastonbury.**

The Pilgrim's Way to Glastonbury

When Joseph and his followers came to England, they probably sailed up the River Parrett and tramped along the ridge of the Polden Hills to Glastonbury. This was the route that became known as the Pilgrim's Way and stretches of it are still visible although the original stones that paved it are mostly covered with grass.

Since so much of Somerset was then under water, the raised causeways were vital and the Polden Ridge would have been a major route. The first place I traced the old way was ironically a short distance above the M5 which now slices through it near Junction 23 above Bridgwater. I left the motorway there and took the A39 towards Street then after 400 yards turned sharp right along the lane at the top of Puriton Hill. The narrow way first runs between gardens and garages and it was difficult to imagine that this was where Joseph and generations of pilgrims had tramped to Glastonbury.

101

To the left through the trees, I saw the misty Somerset plain spread out below, the broad dyke of the King's Sedgemoor Drain slicing across it. I tried to imagine the whole landscape as the silver sheet of water it once was, then followed the track further across a wilderness of old man's beard, rowan and burdock and reached a field overlooking the motorway. In the distance the River Parrett wound lazily towards Combwich, perhaps the place where Joseph disembarked. It was an exciting moment to find among the mundane clutter of lawn mowers, bonfires and bungalows with names like Bali Hai an authentic stretch of the old way.

Retracing my steps, I found the track continued on the opposite side of the A39 running between woodlands behind Knowle Hall. It continues most of the way to Glastonbury, running almost parallel to the present road, parts of it still paved with small stones.

Gog and Magog

Others claim that Joseph took a different route and approached Glastonbury from the south, over Stonedown Hill. If so, he would have passed what was then a magnificent oak grove of which there are now only two survivors. Tradition ascribes this incredible longevity to the two gnarled oaks standing in an ancient lane at the foot of Stonedown.

I walked through Wick and turned right up the lane opposite Norwood Park. After 200 yards, a narrow track branched right and a short distance along it, I found the two oaks, squat, gnarled specimens side by side in a clearing beyond a gate. They are known locally as Gog and Magog, each covered with warts and boasting a massive girth. Although Magog is starting to wither, Gog is still a mass of green and looks good for a few years yet.

Joseph and the Holy Grail

According to legend, Joseph brought with him the Holy Grail, the cup from the Last Supper, and a pair of silver cruets containing

Gog and Magog. ▶

102

Christ's sweat and blood from the Passion. Some say he hid the Grail in a stony nook beneath the waters of Chalice Well on Chalice Hill in the shadow of the Tor. The waters became so reddened with Christ's blood that the place was nicknamed Blood Spring.

These days, the well rises in a beautifully kept walled garden and flows down through a series of pools to a fountain where the water has stained the base bright red. Pedants claim that the striking colour is simply the result of iron deposits but I much prefer the original explanation. The gardens are now tended by a local trust and attract thousands of visitors. I spoke to several, all of whom believed the legend of the well implicitly and one even went on to recount his theories of ley lines.

Many spiritualists are convinced that Glastonbury is the greatest British centre of these mysterious lines of force which can somehow be tapped, yielding great powers for good or evil. The spiral tracks that wind around the Tor are likewise considered highly significant and another man I met at the parish church described a great arc.

The Chalice Well (below) on Chalice Hill in the shadow of the Tor (left) where some say Joseph hid the Holy Grail.

'One of the ley lines passes here. Can't you feel the force?' Deeply ashamed, I had to confess I couldn't though it was not for want of trying.

Like the Grail, the silver cruets have never been found although they are said to be buried with Joseph. No-one is certain where his tomb lies but he was perhaps laid to rest either within the 'Old Church' near his well, a place of healing in the crypt of what is now the ruined Lady Chapel or outside in the southern corner of the old cemetery. Wherever it was, his grave was later filled to a depth of sixteen feet with the bones of saints, monks and kings and was described as 'the holiest earth in England'.

Part of Glastonbury's appeal is the number of unanswered questions it raises and the many different interpretations applied to the history and legend surrounding it. Because of its store of mystery, it attracts, along with the devout and the sightseer, every species of crank imaginable from faith healers to white witches, earnest vegetarians to Pan-worshippers, each desperate to convert you to his particular obsession. But of all their varied and contradictory claims and theories, perhaps the most beautiful belief of all is surely that Christ himself came to Glastonbury.

Christ comes to Glastonbury

> And did those feet in ancient times
> Walk upon England's mountains green
> And was the holy Lamb of God
> In England's pleasant pastures seen?

Few realise that in his great hymn, 'Jerusalem', Blake was writing literally as well as symbolically, describing the widespread belief that as a boy, Christ came to Glastonbury with his great-uncle, Joseph of Arimathea. It is said that long before he came here to preach the Gospel, Joseph sailed to the Westcountry to buy Cornish tin and Somerset copper and lead, bringing his great-nephew Jesus as a shipwright. Although little is written down, there is a long oral tradition that survives in local folksongs. One ballad collected in the 1920s runs:

> **A banner in Pilton Church shows Christ in a boat with Glastonbury Tor behind.** ▶

O Joseph came a-sailing all over the sea
A-trading of metals, a-trading came he.
And he made his way to Mendip
With our dear young Lord.

Gypsies and mummers often sang:

Here come three Josephs, three Josephs are here,
All for to bring 'ee the Luck of the Year.
One he did stand at the Babe's right hand,
One was a lord in Egypt's land,
One was a tinner and sailed the sea.
God keep you merry say we.

The belief had certainly passed into common currency. A banner in the Lady Chapel at Pilton Church shows Christ in a red and gold garment with Glastonbury Tor in the background.

Another hint came in a letter about Joseph and his followers from St Augustine to Pope Gregory the Great: 'God beforehand acquainting them, found a Church constructed by no Human art, but by the Hands of Christ Himself for the Salvation of His People.'

The same idea crops up in the *Life of St Dunstan* which describes the ancient building as 'a church not built by art or man, they say but prepared by God himself for the salvation of mankind, which Church the heavenly Builder himself declared by many miracles and many mysteries of healing he had consecrated to Himself and to Holy Mary, Mother of God.'

These are perhaps references to the tradition that the young Christ, who had trained as a carpenter had helped to construct the building that later became Joseph's Church of Boughs and twisted wattles.

In the Maronite villages of Upper Galilee, many believe that Joseph and Jesus sailed to Britain from Tyre and were stormbound one winter in the west of England. If so it seems entirely possible that the young shipwright would have helped the hospitable local people with whatever work they had in hand.

True or not, it is an enchanting idea and one that everyone would like to believe. Like so many of the legends, it forms a bridge

◀ **Did Christ, when he was a boy, come to England, and to Glastonbury?**

between ourselves and the seemingly grand and inaccessible past. Placing Christ as it does, not only in the exotic Bible lands but among the swamps and green fields of the Westcountry brings him far closer to us emotionally. He is suddenly much more than the kind-faced stranger from long ago and far away, stylised in stained glass. The image of Christ coming to Somerset is both shocking and seductive. It shakes the staid conceptions of Him and lights up the imagination of all who strive to find Him among the shreds and patches of today.

For some, the leap of Faith is achieved, triumphantly and He is once again amongst us:

> Lo, Christ walking on the water,
> Not of Genasareth, but Thames.

Glastonbury Tor from Wearyall Hill. Legends bridge the distance between today and the more mythical past.

Bibliography

Alexander, Marc, *Enchanted Britain.*

Bord, Janet and Colin, *The Secret Country.*

Briggs, Katharine M., *A Sampler of British Folktales.*

Briggs, K.M. and Tongue, R.L., *Folktales of England.*

Chambers, E.K., *Arthur of Britain.*

Hole, Christine, *Saints in Folklore.*

Lawrence, Berta, *Somerset Journal, Quantock Country* and *Somerset Legends.*

Lewis, L., *St Joseph of Arimathea at Glastonbury, 1922.*

Muir, Richard, and Welfare, Humphrey, *Prehistoric and Roman Britain.*

Palmer, Kingsley, *The Folklore of Somerset.*

Peel, J.H.B., *Portrait of Exmoor.*

Simpson, Jacqueline, *British Dragons.*

Tongue, Ruth, *Somerset Folklore.*

Treharn, R.F., *The Glastonbury Legend.*

Whitlock, Ralph, *Somerset Legends* and *Somerset.*

ALSO BY SALLY JONES

LEGENDS OF DEVON
60 photographs and drawings.
Devon is a mine of folklore and myth. Here in a journey through legendary Devon, Sally Jones brings into focus some fascinating tales, showing us that the line dividing fact and legend is an intriguing one.
'...Sally Jones has trodden the path of legendary Devon well...'

Tavistock Times

LEGENDS OF CORNWALL
60 photographs and drawings.
Brilliantly illustrated with photographs and vivid drawings of legendary characters. A journey through the legendary sites of Cornwall, beginning at the Tamar and ending at Land's End.
'Highly readable and beautifully romantic...'

Desmond Lyons, Cornwall Courier

OTHER BOSSINEY TITLES INCLUDE

EXMOOR IN THE OLD DAYS
by Rosemary Anne Lauder

VIEWS OF OLD DEVON
by Rosemary Anne Lauder

KING ARTHUR COUNTRY IN CORNWALL
by Brenda Duxbury, Michael Williams and Colin Wilson

STRANGE STORIES FROM DEVON
by Rosemary Anne Lauder and Michael Williams

DEVON MYSTERIES
by Judy Chard

OCCULT IN THE WEST
by Michael Williams

VIEWS OF OLD PLYMOUTH
by Sarah Foot

AROUND GLORIOUS DEVON
by David Young